Under the Black Waves

By Pierce De Bauche

Copyright © 2025 Pierce De Bauche

North Woods Publishing

All rights reserved. No part of this publication may be reproduced, distributed, or transmitted in any form or by any means, including photocopying, recording, or other electronic or mechanical methods, without the prior written permission of the publisher, except in the case of brief quotations embodied in critical reviews.

Paperback ISBN: 979-8-218-68331-3
eBook ISBN: 979-8-218-68332-0

Acknowledgments

This modern American tragedy draws on extensive research conducted before writing began. Sources for the narrative include records from the FBI and the York County Sheriff's Office, articles and news segments from local and national media, archival game footage from the NFL, and documents from the Boston University CTE Center.

Pierce De Bauche

1

On a cold Sunday in late December 2010, the San Francisco 49ers huddled at halftime in the St. Louis Rams' visiting team locker room. Phillip Adams, a muscular, twenty-two-year-old Black man in his rookie year, gripped his helmet, beads of sweat dripping down his face. He focused on Coach Mike Singletary, a stout, impassioned Black man, as he pointed at the players.

The Hall of Fame linebacker-turned-head coach barked, "I want winners! Winners! We're only up by two points. That won't last long. Now get out there and bury em with a touchdown!"

Phillip strapped on his helmet for the battle ahead. He jogged out with the 49ers in their red-white-and-gold uniforms through the concrete tunnel onto the Rams' field. His heart hammered in his chest, pounding adrenaline through his body. The stadium, filled with tens of thousands of fans, exploded to life as the Rams fans booed and the 49ers fans cheered.

One of those cheering fans, Ashley Clemons, a young Black woman with braided hair, in Phillip's number-35 jersey, urged him on. She shouted, "Let's go, Phillip!"

The Rams team appeared in their blue-and-gold uniforms, and the crowd erupted with excitement. Phillip blocked out the noise as he took his place at the other end of the field. The scoreboard towered over the teams as they prepared to begin the third quarter: Rams 12–49ers 14. Phillip stood at the 25-yard line, one of eleven 49ers special teams players ready to receive the kickoff.

The Rams placekicker, Josh Brown, a tall white man, set the football into position. Brown approached the propped football, his Rams teammates flanking him on each side, and paced out his steps. He ran forward, kicked the ball, and sent it soaring down the field as the Rams players charged after it. The ball tumbled through the air over Phillip's head and the 49ers receiver caught it at the 3-yard line.

As the 49ers receiver rushed with the ball toward Phillip, he prepared to block the descending Rams players swarming around him. The 49ers and Rams players slammed into each other with violent force. Phillip locked onto a Rams player and they shoved each other while the 49ers receiver ran right behind him.

Another Rams player dove at the 49ers receiver but missed and landed on Phillip's left foot instead. Phillip lost his balance as the Rams player he was blocking shoved him over the other Rams player pinning his foot to the ground.

The bones in his ankle shattered, piercing through his skin. He screamed in agony as he fell over. As he landed, the Rams team dogpiled on the 49ers receiver, ending the play. The players pushed and shoved their way back to their feet but Phillip stayed down. His ankle burned with a fiery pain.

The referees sprinted over to Phillip and signaled for the medical teams, who rushed out onto the field. The lead 49ers medic, with his team, reached him first as the Rams medics and referees encircled him. Phillip's anguished eyes peered through his face mask as the lead 49ers medic knelt next to him.

"Phillip, can you hear me?"

"Yeah."

"What's wrong?"

"My ankle. It's broken."

The lead 49ers medic inspected Phillip's left ankle, where his foot dangled to the side, blood pooling onto his white sock. He snapped his head back to the rest of the medics. "Get me a leg cast now!"

One of the 49ers medics sprinted back to the sidelines as the stadium fell silent. Phillip clutched his face mask with both hands. The fire blazing in his ankle became unbearable.

The lead 49ers medic leaned back over him. "I know you're in a hell of a lot of pain, but try to hang on."

Phillip remained silent as he dropped his hands from his face mask. The 49ers medic sprinted back with a leg cast while Coach Singletary followed behind him. Players from both teams removed their helmets and knelt on one knee in solidarity with Phillip, the brutal injury sobering them.

The lead 49ers medic ordered his team to surround Phillip. "This is going to hurt," he said, "but we have to get your shoe off and your leg in the cast."

The medics grabbed Phillip's arms and good leg and pinned them to the ground in a cross, crucified on the field. His bloodstream coursed with adrenaline and cortisol from the fear of losing his foot.

One medic gently lifted his left leg with the broken ankle

off the ground, while another medic carefully untied his shoe and slipped it off his foot. Phillip writhed from the intensity of the pain, but the medics held him to the ground.

They set his leg into the opened black leg cast and sealed it shut. The lead 49ers medic monitored him. "The worst part is over now, Phillip." The Rams injury cart drove out onto the field and pulled up next to him. "We'll get this helmet off you, then we'll load you onto the cart, all right?"

Phillip remained silent, his eyes burning, as the lead 49ers medic unstrapped his helmet and slid it off his head. Phillip closed his eyes and took a deep breath.

"Can you try to sit up for me? We'll move you to the cart."

He slowly opened his eyes. "Yeah."

The 49ers medics grabbed him and picked him up, keeping him stable as they slid him onto the cart.

Phillip sat upright with his left leg extended in the black cast, and the Rams cart driver drove him back to the locker room. The growing applause from the stadium gave him little hope. He stared at the field, broken.

Coach Singletary called out to him, "You're tough as they come, son. You're going to get through this."

Phillip hung his head while his coach, the players, and the fans faded away. His ankle was shattered and so was his career with the San Francisco 49ers.

In the stands, the fans clapped and cheered, except Ashley. Distress weighed her body down. She whispered, "My poor baby."

II

Ten years later, on another cold Sunday in early January 2021, in Fort Mill, South Carolina, just outside of Charlotte, Phillip, thirty-two, lived alone in a sleek, sterile apartment. He leaned forward on his leather couch, dip packed in his lower lip, as the opening ceremony for the Green Bay Packers–Chicago Bears game played on his flat-screen television.

The announcers sat in their booth, welcoming the viewers at home. "For those of you just joining us on this icy day in the Windy City, we have a heated matchup for you."

"That's right, this is a historic rivalry. The oldest in the NFL."

"And it sounds like both teams came to live up to that rivalry today."

Phillip glared as Aaron Rodgers led the Packers onto the field. The game's losses still burned. He grabbed the remote and turned the television off.

The black waves swelled up inside of him and crashed against his thoughts. His chest heaved, the television screen reflecting his snarling face. Lunging to his feet, he stormed around the living room. His tattooed arms tensed as he clenched his fists. The black water pulled him down into the darkness. Seething with rage, he was lost under the black waves.

His body trembled with raw power. The veins in his neck pulsed from the pressure. He took a deep breath and tried to regain control. The black waves receded, and he unclenched his fists, relaxing his hands and letting them fall to his sides. The black waves disappeared, but so did his memory, washed away in the darkness.

That evening, the winter moon streaked across his face through his living room window while he searched the night sky. The cool, white light passed through his skin, exposing his soul. Growing up, he wanted to be alone, to take care of himself, but now he needed his family.

He stepped back from the cold window and the yellow lamplight warmed his face. He picked up his iPhone in a dark-red case from the coffee table, next to his blue can of Skoal chewing tobacco.

He unlocked the phone and placed a call. Alonzo Adams's gravelly drawl answered with surprise. "Hey there, Phil. How you doin?"

"Hey, Dad, I'm alright. You with Mom?"

"I'm with her, just watchin a little TV after dinner. Can I do somethin for you?"

"You have a moment? I wanted to talk."

"Sure. What's on your mind?"

"Well, I bought some land in Rock Hill. Plan on building a house soon."

"That's great news."

Alonzo's voice faded as he spoke to Phyllis Adams. "He says he's fixin to build a house back here soon."

Phyllis's voice called back with delight. "Tell him that's

wonderful, dear. We miss seeing him."

"Phil, you hear that? Your mama says we miss you."

"I miss you too."

"Where you livin at these days?"

"I'm still around here. That's the other thing I wanted to talk to you about."

"What's that?"

"I was wondering if while the house is being built I can move back home?"

"You mean back with us?"

"Just for a little while. I thought I could help you out taking care of Mom too."

"Is that right?"

The question lingered while Phillip waited in silence. Alonzo held his breath, heavy from Phillip's absence.

"Well let me ask her, but I think that should be fine," Alonzo said to Phillip. "He's askin to move back in with us while the house is built," Alonzo told Phyllis.

Phyllis's voice grew louder. "Can I talk to him?" Her warm voice filled the speaker. "Phillip, it's Mom. Now what's this about you wanting to move back here?"

"I thought it'd be nice to come home for a while and help you and Dad around the house, too. I'll make myself useful."

"Is everything okay? We've tried calling, but haven't heard from you in months."

"I'm sorry. I meant to call you back. I've just been busy."

"Well, if you want to come back home, I don't have a problem with it."

"You know I still have P.J. every other weekend?"

"Our grandkids are always welcome." His mom's voice faded away. "Right, dear?"

"That's right, sweetie. The boy's welcome here too."

Phillip's shoulders eased as his mom's voice returned.

"Your dad said yes. You're both welcome here as long as you need."

"Thanks, Mom."

"Now you get a good night's rest and we'll see you soon. Love you."

"Love you, too."

Phillip hung up, the voices of his parents echoing in his head, warming him against winter's chill.

BARREN TREES LINED INTERSTATE 77 under a cloudy sky. Phillip drove his matte-black Camaro down the highway in a black leather jacket over a gray T-shirt and blue jeans. He turned the radio to Charlotte's Streetz 103.3, and the sound system bumped "Last Memory" by Takeoff. The booming bass propelled the muscle car forward.

He only lived half an hour away, but he had forgotten the last time he saw his parents. As he neared home, the tension from wanting to hide increased with each passing mile. He reached the bridge on the Catawba River, the water rushing downstream into the heart of South Carolina.

He turned off the music as he crossed into Rock Hill. The Catawba River drifted away, and the barren trees along the highway revealed Rock Hill High School, the campus set back from the interstate.

He helped the Rock Hill Bearcats win state football and

basketball championships, earning him a football scholarship to South Carolina State University. His high school celebrated his legacy, but the young athlete who walked those halls was gone. Only he remained.

He exited off I-77 and drove down his old neighborhood: a modest, peaceful corner of Rock Hill. He turned down Marshall Road and pulled into the gravel driveway of a small, red-brick house with a white minivan parked in the attached garage. He stepped out of the Camaro parked under the basketball hoop where he used to play with his older brother. A renewed sense of calm filled him as he took a breath of crisp, winter air. He strolled up the front steps and knocked on the door.

Alonzo, a husky, soft-spoken Black man in his mid-sixties, wearing a navy-blue polo tucked into his black pants, opened the door. He grinned at the sight of Phillip, embracing him in a hug.

"There's my son," Alonzo said. "Welcome home."

"Good to see you, Dad," Phillip said, hugging him back.

Alonzo stepped aside and Phillip entered the humble, earth-toned living room with hardwood flooring. Behind the dark-green sofa hung a painting of the Catawba River running through a green valley.

Phyllis, a Black woman in her mid-sixties, wearing a pink sweater and black pants, sat in an electric wheelchair under a wooden cross on the wall. She was paralyzed below the chest but still full of joy.

"There's my baby boy," Phyllis said, her eyes sparkling.

Phillip leaned down to hug her. "Hi, Mom. Good to see you too."

Alonzo and Phyllis studied Phillip who hulked with muscle.

"You look good, Phil," Alonzo said.

"You always worked so hard to take care of yourself," Phyllis said.

"I need to," Phillip said. "It helps me stay focused."

"That's good, baby," Phyllis said, "and you're taking care of yourself outside the gym, too?"

"Yeah, like I said, I'm stayin focused on my next moves, workin on my game plan."

"That's wonderful. We're just happy to see you again."

Phyllis reached out for Phillip's hand and he gave it to her, holding it between her palms.

"We're always here for you. We want you to know that."

"Thanks, Mom. I know you are."

Her touch soothed his old wounds.

In a charming Charlotte neighborhood, Ashley, thirty-two, wearing a leopard-print dress under a jean jacket, packed clothes into her son's red-and-blue Spider-Man travel bag on top of his bed, its quilt covered with images of Marvel's Avengers.

"P.J.," she called out. As Phillip's pickup time approached, her uneasiness grew. Their past fights and failures stirred in the shadows of her mind. She glided out into the living room, decorated with soft, floral paintings. "P.J., you hear me?"

P.J. Adams, a lively seven-year-old, in a blue Adidas sweatshirt and sneakers, watched Pixar's *Soul* while sprawled on the floor.

Allen Hauser, a tall, mellow Black man in his early thirties, sat behind him on the couch. The former college basketball player wore a green-and-purple Charlotte Hornets sweatshirt, covering his tattooed arms, with matching Air Jordan sneakers.

The bright, saturated colors of the animated movie held P.J. and Allen in a trance.

"P.J., I can't find your iPad and your dad is going to be here any minute."

"It's in my room."

"Well, I was just in there and it's not on the charger. Can you help me find it?"

Allen leaned over and patted P.J. on the head. "Go help your mom. You don't want to make your dad wait."

"Okay." P.J. scurried off the floor to his room and Ashley hurried after him. In the hallway they heard a firm knock come from the front door.

"Allen, can you get that?"

"Yeah, Ash."

Allen headed to the front door and opened it to find Phillip waiting. "Hey, Phil. They're coming right now."

Phillip stayed quiet. Resentment silenced his voice.

P.J. sprinted through the house and up to the front door. He ran past Allen and leapt up to Phillip. "Dad!"

Phillip caught him and wrapped him in his arms. "Hey, buddy! Wow, you're getting bigger every time I see you."

P.J.'s love flowed into him, dissolving his resentment.

He set P.J. back down while Ashley approached him carrying P.J.'s Spider-Man travel bag. She set the bag down in front of Phillip and slid back next to Allen. "I just packed it, so you should have everything you need, including his iPad."

"Good deal."

Phillip tapped P.J.'s arm. "I need to talk to your mom quick. Go put your bag in the back seat for me, alright?"

P.J. picked up the bag and lugged it over to the Camaro.

"What do you want to talk to me about?" Suspicion tinged Ashley's tone.

"I thought you should know I'm not living in Fort Mill anymore."

"Where are you staying?"

"I'm back in Rock Hill with my parents for now."

"Is everything okay?"

"Yeah, everything's good. Just wanted to be closer to them."

"That's thoughtful of you."

"I wanted to be closer to my family." The resentment returned in Phillip's voice. "I have some plans in the works too."

"Really?" Ashley's voice fell flat.

"I bought some land on the edge of town. Gunna build a house soon."

"Well, that all sounds nice. I'm happy for you."

Allen put his arm around Ashley. "We're both happy for you."

"Thanks, Allen," Phillip muttered as he walked away.

On the drive back home to Rock Hill, Phillip turned up the radio playing "Fast" by Juice WRLD. P.J. sat in the back in a Batman booster seat, the black-and-yellow bat symbol printed behind him. P.J. pressed his face up against the small back window as the houses streamed past him. Pedestrians and drivers admired the sleek muscle car as it rolled past them.

"Hey, Dad?"

"Yeah, buddy?"

"You have the coolest car ever."

Phillip grinned at P.J. in the rearview mirror. "You think so?"

"It's super cool."

"I think so too."

Phillip revved the engine and P.J. giggled with delight.

"Hey, buddy, guess what? I have a surprise."

"What's that?"

"We're gunna stay at Papa and Nana's house. Are you excited to see them?"

"Yeah!"

"They're excited to see you too. It's gunna be lots of fun. Just you, me, Papa, and Nana."

At home, P.J. played *Rebel Racing* on his iPad while tucked into the dark-green sofa in the living room. He drove a black Camaro down a racing circuit, edging out a white Corvette for first place.

Phyllis drove her wheelchair into the living room from the kitchen, with Phillip following behind her. Phyllis cooed next to her grandchild, "Isn't he just precious?"

"He's my little man."

Alonzo came in through the kitchen carrying a small, white box with a lid on it.

Phillip eyed his dad. "What's in the box?"

Alonzo gave him a wry smile and shuffled over to P.J.

"Hey there, P.J., Papa's got a surprise for you."

P.J. tipped his iPad down and saw Alonzo holding the white box. His face grew with excitement, "That's for me?"

"You betcha."

P.J. took the box and slipped the lid off. He pulled out a small, red football jersey and turned it around to read the name "ADAMS" printed on the back.

"That was your daddy's first football jersey and now it's yours."

P.J. waved it in the air. "My daddy's jersey!"

Alonzo patted him on the shoulder. "Let's see you try it on for size."

P.J. put his blue sweatshirt hood up and held up his arms as Alonzo pulled the red jersey over him and straightened it out. Alonzo stepped back next to Phillip and Phyllis while P.J. admired his new jersey. "Look at that," Alonzo said. "Fits like a glove."

P.J. sprinted through the living room and into the kitchen while pretending to hold a football.

"That boy's got his daddy in him, alright," Alonzo chuckled.

As P.J. sprinted back into the living room, Phillip snatched him by his hood.

"Easy, P.J., no running in the house."

"Can we play catch, Dad? Please?"

"Not today, buddy."

"Why don't you go on and play some catch with the boy?" Alonzo said. "Should still be a bin in the garage with all your footballs and basketballs."

"Please, Dad?"

"Fine, let's go," Phillip grunted.

Phillip and P.J. tossed a small football on the brown, winter grass in the backyard. Alonzo peeked from the porch on the side of the house, watching them fall into a rhythm. His eyes swung back and forth as he followed the ball.

Alonzo shivered from a gust of wind blowing across the yard. He rubbed his arms, smiling at their game, then slipped back in through the kitchen doorway to Phyllis. "Looks like both of em havin a good time," Alonzo said.

In the backyard, P.J. whipped the football to Phillip, who caught it with one hand.

"Hey, Dad?"

"What's up?"

"Give me a hard one. I can catch it."

Phillip pointed down the yard. "Go long."

P.J. took off running and Phillip launched the football across the backyard. P.J. leapt into the air and snatched the ball, pulling it into his chest. He landed on his feet and did a touchdown dance for an imaginary crowd.

Phillip laughed as P.J. trotted back up. "Nice moves, buddy!"

Phillip put his hands up for P.J. to throw him the ball but he held onto it. "Hey, Dad. Can I ask you something?"

"Yeah, what's going on?"

"Do you think when I grow up I can play in the NFL like you?"

"As long as you work hard, you can be whatever you want to be."

"I wanna play in the NFL."

"That's really what you wanna do, huh?" Phillip's smile faded.

P.J. frowned, clutching the football tighter. "Yeah. Don't you think I can?"

"If that's really what you wanna do, then you keep workin at it."

P.J.'s frown eased, loosening his grip on the football. "I will. And I want you to teach me."

"What position do you wanna play?"

"I wanna be a wide receiver."

Phillip smirked. "Oh, so you can score all the points?"

"Someone's gotta do it. Why can't it be me?"

Phillip mean-mugged him and squatted down into position. "Then let's go, hotshot. Try and get past me."

"I can't get past you. You're too good. You played defense."

"Then I guess you're never gunna play in the NFL."

P.J. mimicked his dad and mean-mugged him back. He tucked the ball up into his arm and sprinted around the right side of Phillip. He ran toward the house, but Phillip lunged after him.

"You're not gettin past me!"

"No!" P.J. cried.

Phillip grabbed him with both hands and lifted him into the air while P.J. playfully screamed.

Late that night, while his family slept, Phillip wrote in a black notebook at his desk in his childhood bedroom. Fierce mascots of his favorite teams surrounded him.

A black-and-blue Carolina Panthers poster hung on the back wall, the black panther growling at its challengers. On the left wall hung a green-and-purple Charlotte Hornets poster, the green hornet menacing its opponents. On the right wall hung a black-and-red Rock Hill Bearcats poster, the red beast snarling at its enemies.

Phillip sucked on chewing tobacco while he wrote at a feverish pace. He scrawled rambling thoughts and disconnected ideas, filling pages. Black waves flooded his mind, drowning his thoughts.

On a blank page he drew repeating patterns of diamonds and squares nesting inside each other. He held up the cryptic symbols with manic excitement. His face flashed with paranoia as his eyes shifted around the room. The quiet house listened to him, learning his secrets.

He picked up his notebook and crept across the dark-red carpet over to his large, white gun safe in the corner of his room. He punched in the code and unlocked the safe, swinging the metal door open.

Pistols lined the holsters secured to the inside of the door. Rifles and semiautomatic weapons filled racks in the main body of the safe. Small shelves lined the side compartment, each loaded with boxes of ammunition, except the empty bottom shelf.

There he tucked the black notebook away and closed the metal door.

III

On a cool Sunday in December 2012, in Oakland, California, Phillip, at twenty-four, stood on the sidelines in his black-and-silver Oakland Raiders uniform. The Raiders defense crowded him at their home stadium while the Raiders offense battled the red-and-white Kansas City Chiefs on the field.

Terrelle Pryor, the Raiders six-foot-four Black quarterback, took his position on the field. The Raiders offense lined up in front of him at their own 17-yard line. With thirteen minutes left in the second quarter, the scoreboard loomed over the stadium: Raiders 3–Chiefs 0.

At third down and 7 yards short of a first down, Pryor prepared to make a long throw to avoid punting.

"Ready! Hut!"

Pryor took the snap as the Raiders receivers sprinted down the field. His target, Darrius Heyward-Bey, sped past the Chiefs defense. He crossed the first-down marker, cutting toward the middle of the field. Pryor threw him the football, but it went low. Heyward-Bey reached down in full sprint to catch it, but the football bounced off his fingers and hit the ground.

The momentum in the crowd died as Pryor slunk off the field, the Raiders punter replacing him. Phillip strapped on his helmet as the Raiders punted the football away. A Chiefs receiver caught the football, running it up to their 28-yard line before the Raiders special teams players tackled him.

Lamarr Houston, a Raiders defensive end, rallied his team as they took the field.

"Let's go! Hold the line!"

In the stands, Ashley stood amid the tense crowd in Phillip's number-28 jersey. She clutched her jersey tight, focusing on Phillip as he took the field.

He hustled to his position as a defensive back on the far right side of the defensive line. He positioned his body toward the Chiefs opposing six-foot-four white quarterback, Brady Quinn. The Chiefs running back, Jamaal Charles, braids dangling from beneath his helmet, squatted down behind Quinn. Phillip glared at his targets as Quinn locked into position.

"Hut!"

Quinn took the snap from the Chiefs center and handed the football off to Charles. Phillip knifed through the players as the linemen collided, diving at Charles behind the line of scrimmage. Charles's knee struck Phillip in the head as he collided with him, snapping his head back and knocking him unconscious.

Phillip fell into a body of black water, sinking into the darkness. He choked on the black water as it filled his lungs. He woke up drowning under the black waves, thrashing toward the fading surface light.

Phillip opened his bleary eyes under his black-and-silver helmet. The Raiders defense gathered around him as Lamarr Houston shook him by the shoulder pad.

"Yo, Phil, you okay?"

He glared at the swirling faces, his vision and memory blurry.

The team medics rushed onto the field, surrounding him as the Raiders players stepped back. The lead Raiders medic knelt next to him. "Phillip, what's the matter?"

"My neck," Phillip muttered.

The lead Raiders medic took Phillip's hand. "Can you squeeze my hand?"

Phillip's trembling hand squeezed the lead medic's firm grip.

"We need to follow protocol and get you checked for another concussion right away," the lead medic urged. "Okay?"

"Okay," he mumbled. The black water dampened his thoughts.

"We'll stand on three. One, two, three."

The medics pulled him to his feet, but Phillip slumped over on their shoulders as the ground spun beneath him.

"Easy, Phillip," the lead medic cautioned. "Take it slow."

The medics braced him while he took a soft step forward, the gridiron shifting under his feet. He stumbled off the field with the Raiders medics as small black waves lapped at his mind. He disappeared down the dark concrete tunnel, the faint cheers and hushed concern from the fans echoing off the hard cement walls. The stadium swallowed Phillip alive.

Amid the clapping crowd, Ashley tugged at her jersey in silence. Panic pulsed through her body.

Ashley whispered, "Oh no, not again."

IV

Phillip stepped out of the house in an old sweatshirt, his face masked under an Atlanta Braves cap, sunglasses, and a pulled-up neck gaiter. He mounted his blue four-wheeler parked beside his matte-black Camaro and pulled out of the driveway, seeking the peace of his family's land. He drove past country houses and wooded hills on the outskirts of Rock Hill. The warmth of the midday sun spread over the Carolina farmland.

He rode on to the village of Edgemoor, passing a farmer on a tractor tilling the soil in his field for the next growing season. He turned down Twilight Drive, passing the little white farmhouse his father grew up in. He rode until the paved asphalt ended and a narrow, dirt road began. The tires pressed into the soft, brown dirt as he rolled past the trees lining the road.

He drove the four-wheeler until the forest opened up onto a small plot of farmland, an acre in size, overgrown with weeds. Beside it stood an abandoned barn, tree branches hanging over its weathered roof. A faint creak echoed from its empty stalls. The red paint had long-faded away, like the years when his late grandfather was in good health and ran a prosperous farm.

Phillip pulled down his neck gaiter and surveyed the

weeds, their winter corpses strewn across the fertile soil. He dismounted his four-wheeler and squatted down examining their withered bodies coming back to life, their leaves brittle under his boots.

He dug his hand into the soil, grabbed a weed by its roots, and ripped it from the ground. The cold soil clung to his fingers. Like his father and grandfather before him, he tore into the earth, reclaiming his lost land. He tossed it aside, dug his hand into the soil, found the roots of another weed, and ripped it from the ground.

The soft earth gave way as he knelt. He dug his hands into the soil and kept ripping out weeds, leaving their torn-out bodies in his wake.

He tugged with both hands at a large weed with roots that had grown deep from years of neglect. He tugged until the roots gave way, but as he pulled it out, a scorching heat burst up his back.

He grimaced and stumbled to his feet. He tried to shake off the flames licking his back as he surveyed his work. The uprooted weeds from a small patch of land lay lifeless on the ground. He dusted off his soil-covered hands, hunched over, and rode his four-wheeler back home. The sun lowered into a blaze behind the farmland as the pain blazed within him.

That evening, Alonzo and Phyllis watched WCNC Charlotte Evening News in the living room when Phillip opened the front door, dirt staining his clothes, and stepped inside. Alonzo chuckled as he turned the television off. "Boy, you look like you lost a fight with a pig."

Phillip smirked. "I was down at Papa and Nana's land in Edgemoor."

Phyllis asked, "What were you down there for?"

"I'm starting a garden. Got my patch of land ready today."

"How wonderful," Phyllis said. "I used to love to garden. What do you want to grow?"

"I wanna grow fresh, organic produce. No chemicals or pesticides."

Alonzo grinned in disbelief. "I started playin football to get off that damn farm. But if you wanna till that land nobody gunna stop you."

"I like it out there. It's peaceful."

Phyllis put her hand over her heart. "Jesus said 'God blesses those who work for peace, for they will be called the children of God.'"

"Amen," said Alonzo.

"That's right, Mom. Lord knows I'm tryin, too."

Phyllis studied him, her smile tinged with worry. "Protect what gives you peace, baby. It isn't always easy to find."

Phillip softly nodded, Phyllis's words taking root in his mind.

In the clinic's sterile room, Phillip lay face down on an examination table in a blue hospital gown with his back exposed. The doctor, with her brown hair tied back behind her white coat, lightly pressed her fingers on his vertebrae, starting at the top of the neck.

As she pressed down, he winced. "If it hurts too much I can stop."

"It's fine," Phillip grunted.

The doctor worked her fingers down his back, but when she reached his mid-back he let out a soft groan.

"Are you sure?"

"Yeah."

When the doctor reached his lumbar spine, Phillip let out a deep groan. The doctor, lips tightening, stepped back and waved for him to sit up. "That's enough, Phillip."

Phillip rolled over and sat up while the doctor took a seat across from him.

"The inflammation in your neck and back has become a lot worse. It's in your whole spine, and it's clearly affecting you," she said.

"I can hardly stand it. Most nights it's too painful for me to fall asleep."

The doctor's eyes softened. "I'm going to write you a prescription to help bring down the inflammation. Unfortunately, with these types of chronic injuries to the spine the best thing you can do is try to mitigate the pain."

"I understand." His voice dropped with disappointment.

"But I want you to come back and see me if it gets any worse."

"Thanks, doctor."

PHILLIP DUG A HOE INTO the soil on the farm, dragging it across the ground as he tried to ignore the embers still smoldering in his spine. He tilled the soil until the dark-brown earth spread out in even rows across the garden bed. The damp soil's fertile scent rose into the air, drifting across the farm.

He reached into a black work tote next to him and pulled

out different bags of plant seeds. He squatted, dug a small hole in the soil with his fingers, and opened a bag of tomato seeds.

He tapped a tiny seed into his hand, dropped it into the hole, and covered it with soil. He continued planting up and down his small plot until the embers in his spine heated up and began burning. He stopped and leaned on his hoe as the sound of an approaching vehicle surprised him. A dark-red SUV pulled up next to his blue four-wheeler.

Dwight Sterling, a burly, fifty-year-old Black man with a shaved head under a black-and-blue Carolina Panthers hat, stepped out of the SUV. Phillip, flashing a peace sign, approached him from across the farm.

"What's up, cuz?" Dwight said. "I thought I heard a four-wheeler round here lately."

"Yo, D," Phillip said, "I've been out here gettin a garden started."

He reached Dwight in front of the barn and they shook hands, patting each other on the back.

"Right on. So you're back in town for a while?"

"Yeah, yeah. I just bought some land near here. Plan on buildin a house soon."

"Attaboy. Plantin roots. I'm still just down the road. You should come give me a holler sometime."

"Thanks, D. I will. So what's good with you? Everything good at work and home?"

"Yeah, I'm goin strong. The kids at school are a handful, but I enjoy it." Dwight nodded to the plot of land behind Phillip. "What're you workin on today?"

"I'm gettin my seeds planted."

"You know I used to have a garden out here too?"

"Really? I don't remember that."

"I think you were off playin ball. Took a lot of work keepin those plants alive and well. So you've been warned."

Phillip smirked. "I don't mind. I've got time."

"Can I check out what you've got goin on?"

"Yeah, sure. Come take a look."

They strode over to his patch of land, Phillip pointing to different pockets.

"I've got some collard greens in the back, then some summer squash and tomatoes in the middle, and now I'm planting okra."

Dwight grinned. "It's a good start, but there's a little more to it if you want this garden to prosper."

"Like what?"

"There are a lot of things to think about: how deep you're plantin the seeds, how much water and sunlight they're gettin. Plus the weeds are always a problem."

"I don't wanna use pesticides. I want it to be one-hundred-percent-organic."

"That's gunna take even more work. And those damn deer are gunna love that."

"No, they ain't. I'm not lettin em touch my garden."

"Man, I tried everything," Dwight sighed, "but one day I came out here and saw seven of em tearin up my garden. Destroyed it all."

"Damn," Phillip said.

"I quit gardening after that. Couldn't take it anymore."

"I wanna do this right. I'm not tryin to feed the forest."

"Good luck with that, cuz," Dwight said. "Hope you do better than me."

"Yo, you wanna give it another shot?" Phillip asked. "I could use some help gettin it started."

Dwight lowered his head as he contemplated. "I don't know. Took a lot outta me the first time."

"Word. It's all good."

"You know I'm not coachin wrestlin this year?"

"Nah, I didn't hear that," Phillip said.

"I'm lookin to slow things down," Dwight said. "Thought it was time for someone else to take over."

"I feel you, D. I'll figure it out myself. Always have."

Dwight looked down at Phillip's makeshift garden, then back up at him. "Tell you what, you meet me back out here next Sunday. We'll get these seeds planted right."

"For real?"

"I can make a little time for my kinfolk."

Phillip grinned as the earthy scent of the soil filled his lungs. He stuck out his knuckles and they bumped fists. They would reclaim their land together, starting with the garden.

V

The dim right headlight of the Camaro cut through the darkness on Marshall Road, the left headlight burnt out and black. The beam swept across his brother's and sister's cars parked out front of his parents' house as he turned into the driveway. He slipped out of the Camaro and snuck up the dark front steps, the orange living room lights glowing through the windows.

Lauren Adams, a petite, thirty-four-year-old Black woman, in a black-and-white plaid minidress, sat on the dark-green sofa under the painting of the Catawba River. Alonzo sat beside her, and Phyllis rested in her wheelchair under the wooden cross.

Ryan Adams, a brawny, thirty-eight-year-old Black man, in a gray sweater and black jeans, lounged in a matching dark-green chair. Their lively chatter mixed with the aroma of barbecued chicken, cornbread, candied yams, and fried okra wafting in from the kitchen.

Phillip creaked the front door open, and the living room fell silent. His family fixated on him as he stepped into the house. Lauren rose off the sofa with her outstretched arms, embracing Phillip in a hug.

"There's my baby brother."

"Hi, Lauren," Phillip murmured.

Ryan followed behind her, grinning.

"Been too long, lil bro."

"Yeah, it's good to see you, Ryan."

They gave each other a hug and pat on the back.

"I didn't know you two were comin down tonight," Phillip said.

Lauren smiled and shrugged. "It was sort of impromptu."

"We hadn't heard from you in a while," Ryan said, "so when Mom and Dad told us you were back, we thought we'd come down."

"We've tried calling," Lauren said, "but can't ever seem to catch you."

"I'm sorry. Just have a lot goin on."

Phyllis chimed in, "We told them you're planning on building a house soon."

"I've been talkin with a contractor," Phillip said. "He's workin on the design now."

"That's big. Your own place," Ryan said.

"Gunna be good for you, Phillip," Lauren said.

"Thanks," Phillip muttered.

Alonzo eased off the sofa and shuffled over to Phyllis.

"We been fixin up some dinner, Phil," Alonzo said. "Hope you're hungry."

In the kitchen, the family sat at the table in front of piled plates with their heads bowed in grace.

"Bless this food, Lord," Phyllis said, "and let it nourish our minds, hearts, and souls. In Jesus' name, amen."

"Amen," said Alonzo.

Phillip and Ryan tore into the barbecued chicken while Lauren bit off a piece of cornbread. Alonzo rubbed Phyllis's hand under the lamplight on the old kitchen table, the wood worn down from years of school binders and football playbooks. Phyllis's eyes drifted to Phillip, chewing in silence with his head down, and Alonzo's eyes followed.

Lauren cleared her throat with a sip of water amid clinking utensils before glancing at Phillip. "Next time we'll have to bring the children down like we used to in the summers in Edgemoor."

"My kids been askin to see their kin," Ryan said, turning to Phillip. "What about a weekend when you have P.J.?"

Phillip softly nodded. "That'd be good for P.J. to see his kin."

Lauren faintly smiled as her eyes shifted to Phyllis and Alonzo. "Mom, Dad, you said Phillip's been out at the farm with Dwight?"

"Those two been at it," Alonzo said.

"He's helpin me get a garden started," Phillip said.

Ryan asked, "How's he holdin up?"

"Busy with the schoolkids."

Phyllis's eyes softened. "God bless Dwight. My students could be little hellions."

Alonzo forked a bite of candied yams. "We should call him over too. Your auntie always said Dwight and Phil were two peas in a pod."

"Speakin of Dwight," Ryan said, "I know he's gearin up to watch the Super Bowl next weekend: Patrick Mahomes versus Tom Brady, the young buck versus the old GOAT."

Phyllis swallowed a small bite of fried okra. "Mahomes is talented, but I don't think he can beat Brady, even if he is with the Buccaneers."

"Do you have P.J. next weekend, Phillip?" Lauren asked. "Be like old times. All of us grilling out and watching the game."

"I don't wanna watch it," Phillip muttered.

"Why not?" Lauren asked.

"I'm not feelin it this year."

Ryan nudged him, "You don't wanna see your old teammate, Brady?"

A torrent of black waves rushed through Phillip. "I wouldn't call him my teammate. The Patriots cut me after half a season."

Ryan's smile faded. "You gave it your all in those games, Phil. More than most."

"I guess so," Phillip growled, clenching his fists.

Phyllis murmured, "My baby's been through a lot with that game."

Lauren's voice softened. "P.J. might like watching it with you, is all."

Phillip pounded his fists on the table, "I said I'm not gunna watch it!"

The dishes rattled on the table as his family sat back, holding their breath. Phillip shoved his chair back, storming down the hallway, and slamming his bedroom door shut.

Alonzo leaned forward, the lamplight casting his shadow over the table. He whispered, "Just leave him be. I'll check on him later."

On February 28, 2021, Phillip drove the Camaro down the back highways of Edgemoor on a dreary evening, the winter night creeping in early behind the dark clouds in the sky. He chewed dip while the radio played "Only God Can Judge Me" by 2pac.

An orange Power King tractor stood near the road on a small stretch of farmland, with a "For Sale" sign hanging from the hood. Phillip pulled over to inspect it, adding the sign's number in his iPhone. He headed back to Rock Hill down Reid Road, stopping at the Mount Holly Road intersection. Across the street, he spotted a York County Sheriff's Office Ford Interceptor hidden under the nearby I-77 overpass.

As he made the turn onto Mount Holly Road, the Interceptor pulled out, turning on its sirens and lights. Phillip slowed down and pulled over to the side of the road. The Interceptor pulled over behind him, the sirens fading out while the red-and-blue lights flashed.

Deputy Ryan Quinn, a wiry white officer in his late twenties, stepped out of the Interceptor and marched up to the Camaro. Phillip rolled down his window as the red-and-blue lights streaked through the back windshield and across Deputy Quinn.

"Know why I pulled you over today?" Deputy Quinn asked.

"No, sir."

"You have a burnt out headlight. Looks like your tags are expired too."

"I'm sorry about that. I didn't know."

"I need to see your driver's license and proof of insurance."

"My insurance papers are in my glove box."

Deputy Quinn studied Phillip's grim stare.

"You don't have anythin else in there, do you?"

"No, sir."

"Go on then."

Phillip opened his glove box and took out his insurance papers. He reached into his jacket pocket, pulled out his wallet, and took out his driver's license. He handed them both to Deputy Quinn, who scowled at the documents.

"What's goin on here, Mr. Adams? Your driver's license and insurance are expired, too."

"Must've forgot to renew them."

"You're drivin around with a burnt out headlight in an unregistered vehicle, no valid license, no insurance, and you're tellin me you forgot?"

The shame in Deputy Quinn's voice released a surge of black waves inside of Phillip. He kept his eyes locked on the night sky through the windshield while Deputy Quinn waited for a response. The officer's frame flickered in the red-and-blue lights.

"You been drinkin today, Mr. Adams?"

"No, sir. I don't drink or do drugs."

The black waves flowed through him, a growing rage left in their wake.

"Wait right here then."

Deputy Quinn marched back to the Interceptor while Phillip clutched the steering wheel. The black night sky surrounding him blended with the black water inside of him.

He tried pushing back against the black waves. His breathing slowed and he relaxed his grip. The black waves slowly dissipated into the darkness.

"Mr. Adams." Next to the Camaro, Deputy Quinn held citation papers through the open window, Phillip snatching them from his hand.

"I'm citin you for drivin with a suspended license and no insurance, and for an unregistered vehicle with a faulty headlight."

Phillip squeezed the tickets in his hand.

"You can't be out here drivin like this. It's just reckless. You understand?"

"I understand," Phillip muttered.

"Now go get this taken care of right away. I don't want to catch you back out here till you do."

Phillip nodded while he rolled up the window. Deputy Quinn shook his head while he marched back to his Interceptor. Phillip fired up his Camaro, the shame lingering as he sped off into the night.

VI

PHILLIP PACKED A DIP AT his desk, mania glinting in his eyes as he scribbled down incoherent thoughts. The black waves swirled him around in a whirlpool, pulling him deeper into the dark waters below. A knock on his bedroom door pulled him out of his trance.

"Phil, you busy?" Alonzo asked.

"I'm writing," Phillip grunted.

"Well, you got a letter from the hospital. I'll leave it out here in the kitchen for you."

In the kitchen, Alonzo and Phyllis each drank a glass of iced tea at the table. They studied an old family photo of Ryan, Lauren, and Phillip as teenagers hanging on the wall, when Phillip emerged from the hallway.

"Where's the letter?"

Alonzo pointed to the counter. "Right over there."

Phillip snatched the letter off the counter and tore it open, his lips curling as he read it. "This is bullshit!"

Alonzo's eyes widened. "What's the matter?"

"They're making me pay for everything."

"Who is?"

"The NFL!"

Alonzo and Phyllis flinched as Phillip snarled.

"Take it easy, son," Alonzo said, setting his glass down

with a heavy hand. "Now what's goin on?"

Phillip took a deep breath, suppressing his rage.

"They changed our policy this year. Deductibles went way up. I have to pay for my hospital visits, medications, all of it."

Alonzo glanced at the family photo. "I remember goin down to your games in Atlanta. I know how hard you pushed it. That ain't right."

"I gave them everything. My whole body. And this is how they treat me."

Phyllis shook her head. "It's a sin, treating you like this."

"Some days I hurt so bad I can't even move," Phillip said. "But they don't give a damn."

"I'm so sorry, baby," Phyllis said. "After my car accident, I was able to get disability benefits. Do you know if the NFL has anything like that?"

"They do. Haven't heard anything good about it. But they do."

Alonzo leaned forward, catching Phyllis's eyes. "They owe you that money, son."

Phyllis nodded. "Every last penny. For you and P.J.'s sake."

"They never paid me what I deserved. I can't afford to pay for this shit forever."

"They should be payin for those hospital bills," Alonzo said. "Not you."

"That's the least they could do for me," Phillip said. "The very least."

"You should apply for disability benefits," Phyllis said. "You don't know until you try."

"We'll help you get it sorted out any way we can," Alonzo

said.

Phillip opened the trash can and threw the hospital bill away.

"You're right," Phillip said. "I'm done playin. They're gunna pay up."

Later that afternoon, Phillip roved a wooded trail on his four-wheeler next to the Catawba River. He reached a large evergreen and parked, heading down a footpath to the river. His boots pressed into the soft, wet earth at the water's edge. The river babbled in a soothing rhythm.

He took off his sunglasses and put them on top of his baseball cap. The sunlight glinted off the blue water flowing downstream. His reflection rippled across the river, pulsing under the blue waves. He studied his reflection and met his own eyes watching him.

IN RYAN'S OLD BEDROOM, P.J. sat on the edge of the bed covered in a blue quilt, playing *Rebel Racing*. A poster of a college-aged Michael Jordan dunking in his North Carolina Tar Heels uniform hung on the wall behind him.

Phillip tapped on the open door in the hallway. "Hey, P.J., it's almost bedtime. How about you do a little reading before bed?"

"But I'm almost done with this course."

"You can play again tomorrow, but I want you to read now."

"Fine." P.J. paused the game and slumped off the bed.

"You need to practice if you want to be good. Just like football."

"Will you read with me?"

"Sure, buddy. Get your book and we can read together."

P.J. swapped out his iPad in his Spider-Man travel bag for a picture book. Phillip pushed a pillow against the headboard, but winced as he settled in.

"What's the matter, Dad?"

"Nothin, buddy. Just gettin old."

P.J. tilted his head, eyes tightening. Phillip, forcing a smile, patted the space next to him. P.J. mimicked his dad, pushing a pillow against the headboard and resting against it.

"What book do you have for us tonight?"

The cover of the picture book had a drawing of a young Black boy doing a trick on his skateboard, while his orange cat watched him. P.J. traced his finger across the title in big, purple letters.

"*A Place Inside of Me*," P.J. read, "*A Poem to Heal the Heart*."

"He looks like a pretty cool guy with his skateboard and his little orange cat," Phillip said, patting P.J.'s head.

"He is cool," P.J. said, scooting closer to Phillip as he flipped the book open.

Phillip listened to P.J. read the young boy's story aloud, his heart warming with pride at his son sitting next to him.

The next morning, Ashley stood at the Adamses' front door as P.J. ran to her through the living room.

"Mom!"

"Hi, baby." Ashley bent down to hug him.

"Did you have a fun weekend with your dad?"

"Yeah."

Phillip held the door open with the Spider-Man travel bag

slung over his shoulder.

"Are your parents out?" Ashley asked.

"They're visiting my aunt in Gastonia," Phillip said.

"Well, it's a nice day for a drive. Right, P.J.?"

P.J. nodded along with his mom.

"Time to say goodbye to your dad," Ashley said.

"Bye, Dad."

Phillip rubbed P.J.'s back. "Bye, buddy. I'll see you again real soon, okay?"

Ashley reached out for the Spider-Man travel bag from Phillip.

"I can take that."

"I can walk it to the car for you," Phillip said.

"Thanks." Hesitation hung in her voice.

Ashley took P.J. by the hand, leading him down the front steps to her car in the driveway.

Phillip waited behind her while she strapped P.J. into his red-and-yellow Iron Man booster seat in the back of her car. He handed her the Spider-Man travel bag, and she set it next to P.J., shutting the car door.

"I'll see you in a couple of weeks," Ashley said.

"Hey, wait," Phillip said, "I wanted to ask you something before you go."

"Yeah?"

"When you have a little free time I was wondering if you'd want to come and see the land I bought? It's a nice piece of property near here."

Ashley shifted toward her car door.

"I don't think that's a good idea."

"Why not?"

"I can't do this, Phillip. Not again."

Ashley threw open her car door, but Phillip held it open.

"Wait, Ashley, don't leave."

"Please don't do this in front of P.J.," Ashley begged.

"That's why I am doing this. I love both of you, and I want my family back."

"Phillip, you will always have P.J., but I am not your family."

Tears trickled down Phillip's face. "I need you, Ashley. You've been there for me through so much. My mom's car accident, getting drafted, traveling across the country with me."

"Don't you remember our last year together in Atlanta? How much we fought? I can't do that again."

"Things will be different. I've changed."

"No, you haven't. You keep all your thoughts in your notebook, but you'll never let me in. You've always been that way."

"I'm trying to talk to you right now. I'm trying to let you in."

"It's too late, Phillip. We've grown apart. We're two different people now. We're not those kids we used to be."

"Don't say that. We can work it out if you give me another chance."

Ashley folded her arms. "There's something that I've been trying to tell you—I'm pregnant."

"No! No! No! No! No!" The black waves crashed down and overtook him. "I hate you! I fucking hate you!"

Ashley stood firm, a lighthouse against his storm. "We're

not together. We haven't been for years. You need to accept that and move on."

Phillip stepped back, wiping away his tears.

"Listen," Phillip said, "No matter what happens, I will always take care of you and P.J.—I promise you, I will."

Ashley threw her hands up. "I need to go." She slipped into her car and slammed the door shut.

She cranked the car to life and reversed out of the driveway, P.J.'s terrified face streaming past Phillip. Ashley whipped the car into drive and sped off down Marshall Road, vanishing for another fortnight.

VII

On a hot Sunday in early October 2014, in San Diego, Phillip, at twenty-six, in his all-white New York Jets uniform, took his cornerback position behind the Chargers 46-yard line. Across from him, Philip Rivers, the legendary Chargers quarterback, in his blue-and-white uniform, commanded his team from behind the line of scrimmage. With thirteen minutes left in the second quarter, the scoreboard taunted Phillip: Chargers 7–Jets 0.

The stadium sweltered in the heat, Chargers fans sweating in the sun. Ashley, in Phillip's number-24 jersey, cradled baby P.J. in her arms, rocking him as her breath quickened. "Hold em, Phil," she whispered.

"20! 20!" Rivers hollered.

Phillip squatted down as Rivers prepared for the snap, but Rivers sprinted forward before the Chargers center hiked the ball, while pointing at the Jets defense.

"Hold on, hold on! I want to go 80! 80!"

Rivers dropped back while Phillip's focus shifted to the Chargers receivers flanking the offensive line. The Chargers center hiked the ball, and Rivers took the snap while the Chargers and Jets players collided with each other.

Eddie Royal, a Chargers receiver, cut down the middle of the field, and Rivers threw the ball to him. Royal leapt into the air as a Jets defensive back smashed into him, knocking off his helmet as he caught the ball.

Royal hopped back up at the 22-yard line, his bare head exposed, and beat his chest to the Chargers crowd screaming with excitement. He snatched his helmet off the field as Rivers hurried his team to the line of scrimmage to score a touchdown.

Phillip lined up on the far right side of the field as Rivers prepared for the snap. Across from him, Keenan Allen, a bald-headed Black Chargers receiver, looked past Phillip to the end zone.

"Hut!"

Rivers took the snap while the Chargers receivers sprinted down the field. Phillip stayed in step with Allen while Rivers wound up and launched the ball to him as they entered the end zone. Phillip and Allen leapt into the air as the ball spiraled toward them.

Phillip snatched the ball and pulled it into his chest as he tumbled toward the ground. Another Jets defensive player hit Allen in the air, knocking his helmet off as they fell on top of Phillip.

Phillip shoved himself up, holding the intercepted football to the crowd, while Allen lay speechless. Phillip tossed the football to the referees and trotted to the sideline as the Jets players praised him.

"Hell yeah, Phil! First interception of the season!"

"Rivers is pissed!"

Phillip took off his helmet, his face glowing with joy under the San Diego sun.

In the stands, the Jets fans chanted "Adams! Adams!"

Ashley bounced P.J. in her arms. "You hear that, P.J.? They're cheering for your daddy."

VIII

BEHIND PAPPY'S GUN SHOP IN Edgemoor, locals practiced their accuracy in an outdoor shooting range. Under the shaded pavilion, Phillip loaded a pistol in his shooting booth. He flipped the safety off and pointed it at a human paper target across the gravel field.

The controlled shots ripped through the paper, the bullets burrowing into a sandy mound of dirt behind the fence. He strutted up to the target to inspect his accuracy. Every shot tore through the head and heart. Lethal outside the fenced enclosure.

On his way home, he turned down Saluda Street in Rock Hill, and passed a red-brick strip mall on the side of the road. A sign above a door on the strip mall read "Adam's Frozen Seafood, Meats, & More."

He envisioned himself two years earlier, in 2019, standing in front of the same store. The sign read "Fresh Life Market & More." Near the door, yellow, white, and blue balloons announced Phillip's grand opening. Phillip wore a red athletic shirt, black jeans, and work boots under his Atlanta Braves baseball cap.

From the parking lot, Lauren framed him in her phone camera. "Smile," Lauren said. Phillip grinned and pointed to the Fresh Life sign above his head while Lauren snapped the picture, capturing his joy.

Two years later, Phillip grimaced as he passed the little strip mall. He stepped on the gas and accelerated down the street.

In his bedroom, he punched in the code to the white gun safe and whipped the door open. He holstered his pistol and took out his black notebook from the bottom shelf. He crept outside to the side porch and sat in a porch chair, flipping his notebook open on the table.

The black waves hit him as he started writing, staining his thoughts as they poured out of him. They washed his words away as they pulled him down into the black water below. He turned to a blank page and etched a series of circles inside each other, forming a bullseye. He drew a cross through the center of the bullseye, forming a target. A smile crept across his face as he held the notebook up.

He tossed the notebook on the table and burst out into the backyard. He paced around the perimeter of the yard, the black waves blinding him.

His neighbor, Duane Belue, a white man with salty hair and a goatee, peered out of his back window at Phillip circling the backyard. Duane lingered at the window, his curiosity changing to concern the longer Phillip paced.

THE COFFEE POT GURGLED AS it finished percolating on the hardwood counter in the kitchen. Alonzo pulled out a set of white coffee cups for him and Phyllis, who sat at the kitchen table. Phillip lumbered out of his bedroom in the back corner of the house to the kitchen. Alonzo held up the pot of fresh coffee toward him.

"Mornin, Phil," Alonzo said, his voice warm.

"Mornin," Phillip grunted, rubbing his eyes.

"How'd you sleep?"

"I didn't. Back was killin me all night."

"I'm sorry, baby," Phyllis sighed. "Alonzo, dear, fix him a cup of coffee."

"Sure thing," Alonzo said.

Alonzo filled the cups with coffee, but Phillip waved his hand. "No time," Phillip said. "I'm headin down to Atlanta."

"Atlanta?" Alonzo asked. "Why you goin there?"

"For my disability benefits with the NFL. They want me to see a doctor down there."

"That doesn't sound right," Phyllis said. "Why can't you see your physician in Charlotte? They know your medical history."

"They said it has to be one of their approved doctors. The closest is in Atlanta."

"Atlanta is four hours away," Phyllis said. "I still don't see why you can't see a Panthers doctor in Charlotte. They work for the NFL too."

"They're tryin to play games with me, but I'm not gunna let em win. They forgot who they're messin with."

"That's right, son," Alonzo said, "you keep on pushin back. Now, you gettin a hotel down there tonight?"

"Nah, I'm comin back tonight. I remember the hospital from when I lived there. I'll head back after it's done."

Phillip backed his Camaro out of the red-brick house in the cool morning hours and pulled onto Marshall Road. The late winter sun crested over the roofs in Rock Hill as he drove through the sleepy streets.

When he neared the border between North and South Carolina he turned onto Interstate 85, merging into the morning rush of traffic. He turned on the radio and listened to "Dedication" by Nipsey Hussle as he began his 250-mile trek down into the Deep South.

The drive reminded him of his away games in the NFL: he used the long journeys to focus on his game plan for the battle ahead. His disability benefits were the victory they guarded from him. The radio faded out as he left Charlotte behind. He turned it off and prepared in silence.

He drove over the Lake Hartwell bridge connecting South Carolina and Georgia. A giant blue "Welcome to Georgia" sign with a peach baking in the sun stood mounted next to the interstate. As he edged deeper into Georgia, the memories the state held over him compounded.

Five years earlier, Ashley and P.J. came with him to Atlanta. Phillip and Ashley had been quarreling in New York, and he hoped they would have a fresh start back home in the South.

He pushed himself to have his best NFL season yet, flying high with the Falcons. He brought five years of experience with him, earning over 30 sacks, 6 assists, and 1 interception.

Still, at the end of the season they let him go. He moved back home to Rock Hill with Ashley and P.J., but they brought their feuds home with them. Not long after she let him go too.

He reached Atlanta and roared his matte-black Camaro into heavy traffic. On his way to the hospital he drove past the Atlanta Falcons stadium. Once he called this place his home field, but now he was the visiting team. The opponent determined to defeat them.

In the hospital, Phillip lay face up across a sterile exam bench in a pale green hospital gown with his legs extended.

The NFL physician, a stern white man with gray, receding hair, held Phillip's left ankle as he examined it. A long scar cut across his misshapen ankle joint.

The NFL physician rubbed his hand across the bone and metal. "This is where you feel the pain?" he asked.

Phillip winced, his jaw tight. "Yeah. Even after the surgery it never felt right."

"I can see where the hardware was added."

"It took me almost a full year of rehab."

The physician lifted Phillip's leg higher. "I want you to do a mobility test. Can you extend your foot out, then pull it back?"

Phillip extended his left foot and retracted it, grimacing. "It hurts, but I can do it."

"Can you swivel your foot side to side for me?"

Phillip's ankle ground together until he gave up. "I can't. It hurts too much."

The NFL physician gently set his leg down. "You can sit up now."

Phillip sat up and swung his feet over onto the cold linoleum floor.

"Is there anything else that you want examined for the board?" the NFL physician asked.

"Well, yeah," Phillip said. "I've been having some other problems too."

"Like what?"

"I've been having some memory problems."

The NFL physician tilted his head. "Can you tell me more

about these memory problems?"

"I forget things sometimes. What I'm doing. What someone said. Things like that."

"I see. Anything else besides these memory problems?"

"It's hard to describe. I guess I just feel different."

"Different how?"

"Like something's wrong, but I don't know what."

"I'll put this all down in your medical records, and I'll refer you to a neurologist so they can better examine you. All right?"

"Alright."

Phillip slumped on the hospital bench while the NFL physician filled out his notes on the computer.

Phillip drove animal-repellent stakes into the four corners of his young garden, the motion sensors protecting the sprouting crops with ultrasonic shrieks and flashing lights. The forest surrounding the farm observed in silence.

In the barn, Dwight inspected Phillip's new Power King tractor, when Phillip approached him in the doorway.

"How's it ride?" Dwight asked.

"It ain't the Camaro, but it'll do the trick."

"Man," Dwight said, "you really wanna get the whole damn farm up and runnin again."

Phillip smirked. "And that's just the beginning."

"Oh yeah?" Dwight asked.

"I wanna start another market. But this time it's gunna be different than Fresh Life."

"Wow, for real?"

"I wanna focus on reaching low-income kids. Kids who really need it. You feel me?"

Dwight nodded along. "There's a lot of kids out there that aren't eatin right at home."

"It's important they learn to take care of themselves," Phillip said. "Our health is really all we have."

"Ain't that the truth," Dwight said.

"I can't do it alone though," Phillip said. "I want us to do it together. What do you think?"

"I'm not sure, cuz. Helpin you with your garden is one thing. But startin a market is a totally different animal."

"I'll put up the cash to get it started, but I need you to help me with the farm."

Dwight gazed at the farmland overgrown with weeds.

"You really wanna do this?" Dwight asked.

"Yeah, cuz, I'm serious. You and me. Let's do it."

"Well, shit," Dwight said, a slow grin spreading. "You know I was lookin to slow things down. But I'll have some free time when school's out for the summer."

Phillip asked, smiling, "So you're in?"

"I'm in."

IX

Phillip stepped under the squat rack at the gym and mounted the 405 pounds of cast iron balanced across his back. The weight shook as he stepped back from the rack and found his footing. He glared at himself in the mirror as he summoned his strength.

"For the Night" by Pop Smoke bumped in his headphones as he dropped down into the squat, the bar bending over his back as he hit the bottom. He thrust his hips forward, the veins in his neck throbbing as he powered the weight up.

He grunted as he stepped forward and re-racked the weights. "For the Night" faded out in his headphones to the beeping of an incoming call.

He reached in his gym shorts and pulled out his iPhone, displaying an unknown Atlanta number. He tapped the green icon and took the call.

"Hello?" Phillip asked, his breath heavy.

"Hi, is this Phillip Adams?" a woman asked.

"Yes."

"I'm calling on behalf of your neurology appointment. Are you planning on making your eleven o'clock appointment today?"

"What was that for again?"

"For your MRI. We confirmed the appointment with you last Monday."

"Oh, right. I'm sorry, but I can't make it today."

"I have an opening for the same time next week. How does that sound?"

"Good."

"As a reminder, it's important that you make all your appointments. Otherwise, the doctor can't proceed with your evaluation."

"I'll be there next time."

Phillip ended the call, his disappointed face reflecting back at him in the mirror.

Ashley carried P.J.'s Spider-Man travel bag up the front walkway, her pregnant stomach swollen under her pink dress and white jacket in the warm March evening.

P.J. pounded on his grandparents' front door until Phillip opened it, scooping P.J. into his arms. "Hey, buddy," Phillip said.

Ashley forced herself to march up the steps toward Phillip. She set the travel bag at his feet while he put P.J. down.

"Here you go," Ashley said.

Phillip picked up the bag in silence while Alonzo and Phyllis approached the front door.

"There's my grandbaby," Phyllis cooed.

"Hi, Nana," P.J. said, scooting inside to hug her.

Phyllis gently waved to Ashley. "Hi, Ashley dear. How have you been?"

Her warm voice lulled Ashley's anxiety.

"I'm doing well," Ashley said, touching her stomach. "I'm not sure if you two know, but I'm pregnant."

"Oh my, yes you are," Phyllis said. "And you look lovely in that dress."

"I hope you and the child are in good health," Alonzo said.

"Thank you both. The doctors said everything looks good."

"That's wonderful," Phyllis said. "We're happy for you."

"Well, it was nice seeing you two," Ashley said, "but I better get going."

"Take care now, Ashley," Alonzo said.

Ashley left back down the front steps while Phillip closed the door. He rubbed P.J.'s head, straining to smile. "Ready for another fun weekend, buddy?"

That night, Phillip peeked in the door to P.J.'s bedroom. The poster of Michael Jordan guarded over him while he slept under his blue blanket. He closed the door with a gentle click and slipped back down the hallway past his parents' bedroom and into the kitchen.

He pulled out his prescription pill bottle from his front sweatshirt pocket, and shook a few out. He filled a glass with water from the sink and washed the pills down.

"Phil?" Alonzo called from the living room.

Phillip tucked his pill bottle back into his sweatshirt pocket as he slipped out into the living room.

Alonzo and Phyllis studied their Bibles together under the warm lamplight.

"Is the boy asleep?" Alonzo asked.

"Yeah," Phillip said, "I think I'm gunna turn in too."

"Before you do," Phyllis asked, "do you mind sitting with us for a moment?"

"Is something wrong?" Phillip asked.

Alonzo patted the open seat next to him on the sofa. "We just wanna talk to you, son."

Phillip crept over and sat next to Alonzo under the painting of the Catawba River. Alonzo and Phyllis closed their Bibles as he settled in.

"Now," Phyllis said, "we aren't trying to stick our noses where they don't belong. We just want to make sure you're okay?"

"You mean because of Ashley?" Phillip asked.

"We ain't tryin to pry," Alonzo said, "but after we saw her we wanted to check in."

"Feelings can be a hard thing to let go of," Phyllis said, "no matter how much we might want to."

"When I first found out—it was hard. I got upset. But right now—I'm okay. Okay?"

"I'm sorry, baby," Phyllis said. "If you ever feel upset again you can talk to us."

"I'm tryin to focus on myself right now," Phillip said. "I wanna get this house built. And one day I'd like to have more children too."

Phyllis and Alonzo glowed with excitement.

"We'd love to have more grandchildren," Phyllis exclaimed. "Right, Alonzo?"

"Sure would be nice," Alonzo said.

"I got more plans too," Phillip said. "I was talkin to

Dwight, and he's gunna help me start my own nonprofit."

"What's this now?" Alonzo asked.

"We wanna get the whole farm back up and runnin again. We're gunna grow all-organic produce for low-income kids. Dwight knows people in the school district that can help get us started."

"That sounds like a mighty fine idea," Alonzo said.

"I know I made mistakes with Fresh Life Market, but I learned from them. This time it's gunna be different."

Phyllis tapped the cross on the cover of her Bible. "I've been praying every day for God to show you the way."

"Your mama and I both been prayin for you."

"I have a good feeling about this," Phillip said. "We're gunna make it happen."

"Never forget, son," Alonzo said, "you're part of a special group of men. You can do anythin you put your mind to."

"Thanks, Dad," Phillip said, softly smiling.

Alonzo leaned back in the sofa, a grin sweeping across his face. "I'll never forget the game you picked off Peyton Manning. We told everyone at church the next Sunday. Didn't we, sweetie?"

"Oh, yes, your dad told the whole congregation. Most of them watched your games live, but he was just so proud of you. He wanted everyone to know."

Phillip smirked. "That was my first year with the Raiders."

Alonzo put his hand on Phillip's shoulder. "If you can pick off Peyton Manning, you damn sure can do this."

A BACKLIT SCREEN ILLUMINATED AN MRI of Phillip's brain. Soft, liquid brain matter compressed into a two-dimensional image.

The NFL neurologist, a middle-aged white man, studied the brain scans, his glasses and beard hiding his discerning glare. "I don't see any signs of tumors or lesions," he said. "There are no signs of inflammation either."

Phillip nodded along, his eyes transfixed on the images of his brain.

"Can you try to describe anything else about what's bothering you?"

The images lost their hold over him as he shook his head.

"It's like a black wave washing over me. I try to resist, but it's too strong."

"And that's when you have memory lapses and lose control?"

"It feels like I'm drowning. Under the black waves."

The NFL neurologist scratched his beard, processing his description.

"Unfortunately, our current technology doesn't allow us to test for everything."

"What's that mean?" Phillip asked.

"In your medical history, it says you sustained two concussions in three games when you played for the Raiders. Correct?"

"I've had concussions from playing since college."

"You could be feeling the onset of CTE," the neurologist said, his voice cold. "Although that can only be diagnosed postmortem."

"So there's nothing else you can do?" Phillip asked.

"Not at this time," the neurologist said. "Your records also show you were seeing a therapist before you retired. If your problems get worse I would recommend seeking out more therapy."

"All right," Phillip sighed. "What's next?"

"I'll submit my evaluation to the board, and from there they will make a decision."

X

On a humid Monday in late July 2016, Phillip, at twenty-eight, stood on the sidelines of the Rock Hill High School football field. The young high school players, in black-and-red practice jerseys, thronged around him as others scrimmaged on the field.

Coach Percy Sutton, a bald, powerful Black man, paced on the sidelines. The Bearcats head coach and military veteran hollered at the players in his low, Southern drawl.

"Come on, now. Line it up and let's go again!"

Phillip clapped his hands. "Let's go, defense!"

The players on the sideline whispered to each other as Lauren hurried toward them on the far side of the field. Phillip, surprised, rushed over to meet her before she reached the players.

"What are you doing here?" Phillip asked.

"Where's your phone? You have like a hundred missed calls. Everyone's looking for you."

"Why?"

"The Colts want you to try out for them tomorrow. Your agent has been calling everyone in the family trying to get a hold of you."

On the field, a young quarterback lobbed a pass to a receiver. As he caught the ball a linebacker slammed into him, tackling him to the ground.

"Did you hear me?" Lauren asked. "You gotta go right now."

"I'm not going," Phillip said.

"What? Why?"

"I don't want to."

"Why not?"

"I have to get back to practice."

Phillip tried to leave, but Lauren grabbed his arm.

"Wait. I'm getting Dad on the phone. He's the one that sent me down here looking for you."

Lauren whipped out her phone and dialed Alonzo, his gentle drawl cutting through the sticky, summer air.

"Lauren, you find him?" Alonzo asked.

"Yes. And you need to talk to him. Here he is."

Lauren shoved the phone into Phillip's hand.

"Phil, are you there?" Alonzo asked.

"Yeah," Phillip said.

"Your sister tell you? Scott Casterline got you a tryout with the Colts, but you gotta catch a plane at 6 p.m. tonight. He already bought the plane ticket, all you gotta do is get there to the Charlotte Airport on time."

"I'm not going," Phillip muttered.

"What are you talkin about?"

"I don't wanna go."

"Why not? That don't make any sense."

"I just don't."

"But, son, are you sure about that?"

"Yeah, I am."

"Listen," Alonzo said, "I want you to think really hard about this. If you change your mind, the ticket is already bought. All you gotta do is catch the 6 p.m. flight to Indianapolis. Alright?"

"Alright."

Phillip pulled the phone away and ended the call. He gave Lauren her iPhone back, leaving her stunned as he rushed back to the high school football players.

ALONE IN HIS APARTMENT, PHILLIP journaled in his notebook at the kitchen table, the golden rays of a setting sun streaking in through the kitchen window.

> *She says she wants me to open up more. But I don't know what else she wants me to say that she doesn't already know. It makes me angry, and then she gets angry. I can't keep her happy. She gets upset about everything. If a girl throws herself at me she gets really upset. I tell them no and I have a girlfriend, but she says I like it. I don't know what else she wants me to say or do. I don't like fighting in front of P.J. and neither does she. That's why she says she wants to take a break. I don't want to lose her. But we can't keep fighting all the time. It's not good for us or him.*

Next to his notebook his iPhone vibrated, displaying an incoming call from Scott Casterline. Phillip set the pen down and stood up as he answered the call, the golden rays of light shining on his face.

"Hi, Scott."

"Phil, I've been trying to reach you all day," Scott

exclaimed, his voice fatigued. "Where have you been?"

"I'm sorry. I was gunna call you back."

"I already talked to your family. Why didn't you go?"

"I did go. I tried to make the flight, but it already left."

"They said you didn't want to."

"Nah, I changed my mind. I tried to go. They said I missed the flight, and there aren't any more flights tonight."

"Damn," Scott sighed, "it's too late now. They needed you there tomorrow."

Phillip stood by the window, the golden light dimming to dusk.

"Can I ask why you didn't want to go when you first got word?" Scott asked.

"Because we both know how this was gunna play out."

"What do you mean?"

"I just played my best season in Atlanta. And they still cut me."

"That was their mistake, and the Colts knew that. It could've been different with them."

"It was gunna be the same old shit," Phillip said. "I played for six teams in the last six years. Each season I played better, and each season they still cut me. I'm tired, Scott. I don't wanna do it anymore."

"So I guess that's it then."

"Yeah," Phillip said, "I guess it is."

XI

IN THE GARDEN, DOZENS OF weeds sprouted between the growing crops. Phillip thrust his hoe in between a row of okra plants, sweat clinging to his red-and-blue South Carolina State Bulldogs T-shirt, tearing them out by the roots. On the other end of the garden, Dwight drove his hoe in between the squash, beads of sweat dripping down his face.

"People think you hoe once and then you're done," Dwight huffed. "But that's where they're wrong. You gotta keep killin the weeds or the crops will die."

"And that ain't—" Phillip grimaced as a fire ignited up his spine. He leaned on his hoe as Dwight rushed up to him.

"What's wrong?" Dwight asked.

"My back. It's killin me," Phillip grunted.

"Let's take a break and cool off. I'm gettin stiff too."

Phillip hunched over to a log and squatted down. Dwight hunkered down next to him, their caps' shadows cutting across their faces in the hard light of the high sun.

"You know," Dwight said, "we can always pick it back up again tomorrow."

"Nah," Phillip said, "give me a minute and I'll be good."

"Right on, cuz."

A Carolina chickadee, a small songbird with a black-and-white head and a gray-and-white body, perched on a tree branch near the garden. Another Carolina chickadee fluttered through the air and perched next to it.

They sang their song in turns, a long four-noted whistle, over the farmland. The first Carolina chickadee spread its wings and hopped off the tree branch. The second Carolina chickadee followed, flying together across the trees toward Rock Hill.

As the chickadees disappeared, Phillip pointed toward the trees. "Hey, you see down the road there's some land for sale?"

"Yeah, I saw that," Dwight said.

"I'm thinkin about buyin it."

Dwight's eyes widened. "You want to expand already?"

"I wanna make this happen. Don't you?"

"I thought you'd wanna see how we do here first."

"I'm ready for more," Phillip said. "Unless you think I should hold up?"

"If that's what you wanna do, cuz, go get it."

"I'm gunna."

Phillip envisioned acres of farmland ready for harvest.

"I saw Coach Sutton at school the other day," Dwight said.

"Oh yeah?" Phillip muttered.

A flood of black waves drowned out his vision.

"I told him you were back in town. He said you should give him a holler if you wanna help this summer with football camp."

"Can't do it this year. Got too much goin on."

"I know you got a lot cookin, but those kids really look up to you. And you're good with them."

Phillip clenched his fists. "They'll be fine without me."

"You should think about it. Even once a week would mean a lot to the team," Dwight said.

Phillip's fists tightened, glaring at the weeds choking his garden.

"P.J.'s gettin pretty big now. I bet he'd love to come with you and watch the high schoolers practice."

"You hear me? I said no!" Phillip shouted.

Phillip grabbed his hoe and stomped back to the garden. Dwight pulled his cap down and trailed behind Phillip as he stabbed his hoe into a patch of weeds.

Ashley waited in her doorway in a flowing yellow dress as P.J. sprinted up the walkway to her. "Hi, baby. Give me a hug."

Phillip, with the Spider-Man travel bag slung over his black leather jacket, eased up the walkway while they hugged. Ashley let go of P.J. and met Phillip smiling down at them, the tension diffusing under the soft, spring light.

From behind Ashley, Allen loomed in the hallway, his eyes tight on Phillip. Ashley patted Allen's chest until he focused on her.

"Can you take P.J. inside for me?"

"Yeah, Ash."

"Come on, P.J.," Allen said, waving him inside. "If you hurry there's enough time to watch a movie before bed."

"I want to watch *Black Panther*."

Ashley and Phillip watched them disappear down the hallway and into the living room.

"He really does love P.J.," Ashley said, softly smiling.

"That's why he wanted another child."

"I can tell he treats him right," Phillip said.

"We're planning a vacation to Miami soon. But we wanted to make sure it's okay with you first before we told P.J.?"

"That sounds nice. When do you want to go?"

"In the beginning of April when he's off school for spring break."

"Spring break in Miami? Don't you think he's a little too young for that?"

Phillip winked at her.

"It won't be like that," Ashley laughed.

"I hope you have a nice time."

"Thank you, Phillip."

Phillip slid the Spider-Man travel bag off his shoulder and handed it to her.

"Better give you this before I go."

She took the bag from him and stepped back inside.

"Have a good night," Ashley said, closing the door.

Phillip drooped back to his Camaro, and drove back home through her quiet neighborhood. "Falling Down" by Lil Peep and XXXTentacion played on the radio while Phillip pulled back onto I-77 to Rock Hill. Phillip cranked the volume up, the melody muting his thoughts.

At home, Alonzo and Phyllis waited in silence as Phillip opened the front door.

"What's goin on?" Phillip asked.

His boots thudded against the hardwood floor as he approached them.

Alonzo pointed to a letter on the coffee table. "You got a

letter from the NFL Players Association."

Phillip snatched the letter off the coffee table and tore it open. He pulled out the letter and skimmed through the text.

Each word of their rejection crashed harder and harder against his thoughts, stirring a storm of black waves inside of him. He threw the letter, the papers scattering across the hardwood floor.

"What's it say?" Phyllis asked.

"They denied me all of it. I'm not gettin any benefits."

"We're sorry, Phil," Alonzo said. "We know how much you're hurtin."

"Can you fight it?" Phyllis asked. "What about an appeal?"

"They don't care about me," Phillip growled. "They're not gunna change their mind."

"Now, son, come over here and sit down," Alonzo said.

Phillip swayed from the storm of black waves swelling inside of him.

"I know you're mad as hell," Alonzo said, "but your mama and I want you to listen to us."

Alonzo patted the sofa next to him, an island to take refuge. Phillip thudded over to the seat and dropped onto the cushion.

"We were worried this would happen," Phyllis said, "but you're going to get through this."

Phillip held his head in his hands. "It feels like the whole world is against me."

"We're not against you, Phil," Alonzo said. "All your kinfolk are there for you too."

"Now, baby," Phyllis said, "I want you to listen to me."

Phyllis, under the wooden cross, calmed the black waves in him.

"When my car spun off the road and I broke my back, I thought I was going to die. I was so scared. And in so much pain. But I knew in my heart it wasn't my time yet. God needed me here for my family."

"Yes we do, sweetie," Alonzo said.

"As hard as those first few years were," Phyllis said, "I found a way to keep going. And now I'm just so thankful to God he spared my life that day."

"I am too, Mom," Phillip said. "I don't know what we'd do without you."

Alonzo patted Phillip's shoulder. "I know you're in all kinds of pain I can't even imagine. But long-distance truckin gave me my fair share of problems too."

"I know you always worked hard, Dad."

"Even when I was your age I was havin back problems from drivin so much. I saw Doctor Lesslie about it. You know him from down the road?"

"Doctor Lesslie," Phillip said. "Yeah, I know him."

"He's the founder of Riverview Family Medicine. I used to go there when I was younger. He tried to do some work on me, but it didn't help me none."

Alonzo leaned forward and rubbed his lower back.

"It's still hurtin me all this time later, but I found a way to keep goin. Just like your mama did. Just like you will too."

Phillip lay castaway on an island, a black ocean surrounding him.

XII

"Football City USA" hung in red letters on a blue banner over Main Street in downtown Rock Hill. Phillip cruised his matte-black Camaro under the banner, one of nearly two dozen NFL players to come from the city of 75,000 people, the most per capita in the country.

On Cherry Road, he pushed open the door to Nirvana Smoke Shop. A scruffy white clerk waited behind glass shelves filled with smoking pipes and bongs. The speakers overhead played "What's the Use?" by Mac Miller.

"Welcome to Nirvana. How can I help you?"

"I'm lookin for some kratom," Phillip said.

"I got you covered. You want capsules or liquid extract?"

"Which one is better?"

"The capsules are stronger, but the liquid extract hits quicker."

"I'll take both."

"You got it."

The clerk slid a package of kratom capsules and liquid extract off a rack behind him.

"It's a shame it's banned in some states," the clerk said. "Just make sure you're taking the right dose."

"I will."

In the Camaro, Phillip popped open the kratom bottle

and dumped a few gold capsules into his hand. He cracked open the liquid extract and washed the gold capsules down with the black liquid. He drove to Edgemoor, sloping through the back highways, as the sedative cooled the fire burning throughout his body. Charlotte's Streetz 103.3 played "Armed & Dangerous" by King Von.

On Tinkers Creek Road, he pulled into the parking lot of Pappy's Gun Shop and popped his trunk. Under the shaded pavilion, Phillip gripped a 9mm pistol in his shooting booth. He faced off against his human paper target. He unloaded a rapid round of bullets across the gravel field, shredding the paper. Numbed from the kratom, he strutted up to the target to inspect his accuracy.

Every shot tore through the head and heart. Still lethal outside the fenced enclosure.

BLACK STARS SURROUNDED A BLACK crescent moon on Phillip's white notebook page. He inked in another black star while sucking on chewing tobacco. The dark tidal force pulled on the black ocean within him, bringing a rising tide of black waves to the surface. Phillip leaned back from his desk and closed his eyes, while the black waves swallowed him whole.

Next to his can of Skoal, his iPhone vibrated from an incoming call from Ashley. His eyes cracked open to her name pulsing on his desk. He picked up the iPhone, answering the call.

"Ashley?" Phillip muttered.

"Where are you?" Ashley asked. "P.J.'s waiting for you."

"Huh?"

"You're taking him this weekend, right?"

"I can't."

"What do you mean you can't?" Ashley whispered.

"I just can't."

"You know how much he looks forward to seeing you. He's really going to be hurt if you don't show up."

"I'm not feelin good. Tell him I'm sorry."

Phillip pulled the phone away and hung up on her. The undertow from the black waves dragged him to the trenches of the black ocean's floor. He shoved his chair back and stormed out of his bedroom.

At the kitchen counter, Alonzo brushed red barbecue sauce onto pork ribs. Phyllis sat in her wheelchair at the table, her smile fading as Phillip stormed past them.

"Hey there, Phil," Alonzo said. "You off to get P.J.? I hope the boy likes ribs."

"I don't have him this weekend. He's at a sleepover."

"Oh. Well, that's good the boy is makin friends."

"I'm headin out," Phillip said. "Have a good night."

As Phillip stormed out the door, Alonzo glanced back at Phyllis softly shaking her head.

Outside, the neighborhood turned crimson under the red, setting sun. He fired up the four-wheeler and tore out onto Marshall Road.

Phillip roved through the dark forest next to the Catawba River. The red sunset bled over the night sky, staining the blossoming flowers on the trees to blood-red. Long, black shadows streaked across dead leaves on the trail as he roved deeper into the dark forest.

Phillip parked next to the silhouette of a large evergreen, creeping down the footpath to the river. His boots sank into the black earth as he neared the water's edge. The black river chanted in a hissing whisper.

The red light of dusk flashed off the coursing water. His shadowy reflection rippled across the black waves pulsing with bloody light. The red sun died behind a black wall of trees across the river, the last crimson flashes of light fading into the night.

In the darkness, Phillip crept back up the footpath to his four-wheeler. He fired it up, powering on its front headlight. He prowled alone through the black forest, a creature of the night.

He drove back home down Marshall Road, but he passed his house and drove west. He passed an open field with the night sky expanding over it. The faint light of the crescent moon and stars glowed too pale to penetrate the black waves raging in him.

His headlight brightened white fences protecting extravagant, country houses, with rows of trees shielding their wealth from view. Further down, his headlight ran along a brown, wooden-beam fence on the right side of the road, until it reached a stone archway at the edge of a long driveway.

He switched off his headlight and cut up the private drive, following rows of trees lining the path. At the end of the driveway, a metal gate barricaded a sprawling, brick mansion.

Phillip powered on his headlight, exposing a placard on the metal gate reading "Lesslie." He scowled at the name before switching off his headlight and creeping back down the driveway.

XIII

In his bedroom, Phillip tossed back pills with liquid kratom, packed a dip, and rested on the edge of his bed. The mix of chemicals calmed him as the beasts on the walls charged him from all sides.

On his desk, his iPhone vibrated through the silent room. He reached over and answered an incoming FaceTime from Ashley, his eyes heavy from the medication.

P.J. appeared on the screen, his dewy eyes glowing through the phone. "Hi, Dad."

"Hi, buddy," he muttered.

"Where are you?" P.J. asked.

"I'm at home."

"When are you coming to get me?"

"I'm sorry, buddy. I can't this weekend. I'm sick. I thought your mom told you."

"I tried telling him," Ashley said, her face appearing behind P.J., "but he wanted to talk to you."

"You didn't come get me last time either," P.J. said.

"I know and I'm really sorry. I'm tryin to get better."

"Don't you wanna see me anymore?" P.J. asked.

"Of course I do. And I'll make it up to you as soon as I feel better. I promise. Okay?"

"Okay."

"I gotta go now," Phillip said. "Have a good weekend. I love you, P.J."

"Love you too, Dad."

Phillip hung up and tossed the phone on his bed.

He slumped over to the white gun safe, and pulled out his black notebook. He lumbered out of the house to the side porch, sliding the door shut behind him, and closed himself off to a quiet corner of the yard.

As he set his notebook down on the table Alonzo opened the porch door.

"Hey there, Phil."

Phillip's body tensed. "Hi."

"No P.J. again this weekend?"

"He's at a birthday party."

"Uh-huh," Alonzo mused. "You writin again?"

Phillip nodded in silence.

"What you always writin about anyhow?"

"I'm writing a book."

"Now is that so?"

Phillip nodded in silence, pulling out a chair and settling into his seat.

"It's a nice spring day," Alonzo said. "Your mama and I were thinkin about goin for a drive. We're wonderin if you wanna come along?"

"I'm fine," Phillip muttered.

Alonzo shuffled over to the table, pulling out a chair and settling in next to him.

"We were hopin to see the land you bought for your house. Your mama wanted you to take us there. What do you say?"

Phillip sat in silence.

"She was really lookin forward to it," Alonzo said. "You know she don't get out much."

"Alright," Phillip mumbled.

In the white minivan, Alonzo drove while Phillip sat in the passenger seat. Phyllis, strapped in her wheelchair, rode in the emptied-out body of the vehicle.

They hummed through Rock Hill toward Edgemoor, the houses giving way to a hilly landscape. Phillip pointed to a large plot of land dotted with trees.

"This is it."

Alonzo pulled the minivan over and parked, admiring the lot.

"This sure is a pretty piece of land you got here, Phil," Alonzo said. "Say, sweetie, can you see it alright back there?"

"Yes," Phyllis said, "and it looks wonderful. I haven't been out here in ages, but I always loved this area."

"It's quiet out here," Phillip said. "A man can be at peace."

"That's right, son," Alonzo said. "Nothing like your own place."

"Do you know when you plan on starting construction?" Phyllis asked.

"I don't have a date yet," Phillip muttered. "I need to call the contractor back."

"It's okay, baby," Phyllis said. "I was just curious."

"Yeah, Phil," Alonzo said, "we like having you back home. We ain't tryin to rush you."

"I can tell you it's gunna be a big house," Phillip said. "And

I'm gunna build a basketball court too, so P.J. can hoop whenever he wants."

Phyllis gently smiled. "I know P.J. is going to love it out here."

Phillip envisioned playing a one-on-one basketball game with a teenage P.J. on the land in front of him, the future glimmering in his eyes.

"That's my plan," Phillip said. "Things are about to change. I can feel it."

"We know things ain't been easy for you," Alonzo said, "but you're gunna pull through. You always do."

"I was wondering," Phyllis asked, "have you had a chance to look into an appeal?"

"Not really," Phillip said. "I've been busy. And like I said, I don't think there's much point."

"We know, baby," Phyllis said. "We just want them to pay you what you deserve."

"They will. I'm not done with them yet."

BEHIND PAPPY'S GUN SHOP, PHILLIP gripped a .45-caliber Kriss Vector semi-automatic rifle with a tommy-gun-style drum magazine. He aimed the weapon of war with both hands at a human paper target. He squeezed the trigger and the metal drum unloaded a spray of bullets, eviscerating the paper target.

He set the Kriss Vector down on his table, exchanging it for a 9mm MP5 submachine gun. He strapped a magazine in, tucking the butt of the gun in his shoulder pocket. The mangled human paper target clung to life before Phillip unloaded a second spray of bullets, annihilating its remains.

In the parking lot, Phillip marched to his matte-black Camaro, the guns slung over both his shoulders forming a metal cross. He unlocked the trunk, laid the guns down, and closed the lid, when he felt the pulse of an incoming call from his iPhone.

He pulled the dark-red iPhone out in the quiet parking lot, the incoming call from Scott Casterline surprising him.

"Scott?" Phillip answered.

"Hi, Phil. How's my favorite client doing?" Scott's confident charm rang through the speaker.

"I'm alright."

"Say, I wish I was calling under better terms. But I heard you've had some setbacks with the NFL Players Association?"

"Who told you that?"

"Your parents called me and told me what was going on."

"I'm takin care of it."

"They're just trying to look out for you," Scott said. "And as your agent that's my first priority."

"I know."

"I'm going to have my assistant send you over a few links to other resources. It might not be exactly what you're looking for, but I think they'll help."

"Alright, thanks," Phillip muttered.

A blue Ford F-150 drove past the parking lot down Tinkers Creek Road, its rumbling engine filling the air.

"I know we don't keep up as much as we used to," Scott said, "but if you need anything don't hesitate to call me. I always have your back."

"I know you do."

"You're going to get what you need. I'll make sure of that. Alright?"

"Yeah, alright."

"I'll talk to you soon, Phil. Take care."

Phillip hung up and slid into his Camaro. He accelerated out of the parking lot onto Tinkers Creek Road, the speakers blasting "Ready to Die" by The Notorious B.I.G.

He left target practice behind in Edgemoor, and prepared for the real target in Rock Hill.

XIV

THE FLOWERING OKRA PLANTS GREW as tall as Phillip. Their broad, white flower petals with a purple center radiated out from a long, white stigma. Behind the flashing animal-repellent stakes new weeds sprouted between the okra stalks.

He circled around the okra to the rest of the garden where more weeds filled the soil, strangling his crops with their roots. Green tomato bulbs and young summer squash laid smashed and half-eaten on top of the weeds. The collard greens were uprooted and chewed down to the stalk.

"Damn it," Phillip muttered as he scanned across the quiet, weedy farmland. A gust of wind blew through the forest, shaking the white okra flowers.

He bent down to pick up a smashed tomato, but the spinal fluid in his back turned to lighter fluid, erupting from a spark of inflammation. He grimaced as he straightened up, hobbling toward the dirt road.

He crawled on top of the four-wheeler, the flames engulfing his spine. He tore out of the farm, the spring trees whirring past him as his inner flames drove him faster. Phillip accelerated down Twilight Drive as Dwight exited his house. Dwight threw his hands up waving to Phillip, but he sped past him down the street.

Phillip brought the four-wheeler to a hard stop where

Twilight Drive ended, the off-road vehicle rumbling in place. He pulled the handlebars to the side and turned around. Dwight glared at him as he pulled up into Dwight's driveway.

"What's your problem?" Dwight asked. "You're just gunna blow past me like that?"

"My bad," Phillip said. "I had somethin on my mind."

"Everyone's been tryin to reach you," Dwight said, "but you're not answerin your phone."

"Is somethin wrong?" Phillip asked.

"Aunt Shelly died."

"Oh no," Phillip sighed. "I'm so sorry to hear that."

"I talked to your sister," Dwight said. "Sounds like your dad is takin it pretty hard."

"Is he at home?"

"They're all at Atrium Health in Charlotte," Dwight said. "I was seein if you wanna go with me?"

The week before Palm Sunday, silence hung over Robinson Funeral Home as Alonzo opened the front door to the chapel. Phyllis drove her wheelchair inside the white room while Phillip and Alonzo followed behind her. Under soft, filtered lights, friends of Shelly and the extended Adams family filled the pews. Lauren, Ryan, and Dwight each filled a row with their families.

Ahead of them, Shelly Mae Adams, a Black woman in her early seventies, lay in her white casket adorned with white lilies. Phillip stiffened at the sight of his deceased aunt until Alonzo tapped him on the shoulder.

"Let's go pay our respects."

Phillip trailed behind Phyllis and Alonzo down the center aisle, past rows of families eyeing him, a local football legend, until he reached the white casket. Phillip hardened as he hovered over her lifeless body. Alonzo and Phyllis softened, moved to tears.

"She was such a kind and lovely woman," Phyllis whispered. "I couldn't have asked for a better sister-in-law."

"Thank you, sweetie," Alonzo rasped, wiping a tear from his eye. "I know she felt the same about you."

"I'm sorry, Dad," Phillip muttered.

"Thank you, son."

Alonzo rubbed Phyllis's shoulder. "Ready, sweetie?"

Phyllis gently nodded.

"Well, Phil," Alonzo said, "I think we're gunna go sit with Dwight and his folks."

Phillip turned back to the chapel, the attendees gently smiling and waving to him, little boys leaning over their seats in awe. Phillip dropped his head, sneaking past the adoring fans to the back corner of the chapel.

Lauren slipped away from her family, smoothing out her black dress as she approached him. "Mind if I sit with you?"

"Sure."

Lauren settled into the seat next to Phillip while he kept his head down.

"How are you managing?" Lauren asked. "I know it can be overwhelming sometimes."

"Yeah, I'm okay," Phillip mumbled.

Lauren leaned back in her seat, somber murmurs drifting through the chapel.

"How's P.J.?"

"He's good."

"He's with Ashley today?"

"Yeah."

Dwight glanced at them and nodded as Lauren smiled back.

"You and Dwight still working on the farm?" Lauren asked.

"Uh-huh."

"Aunt Shelly used to work with daddy out on the farm."

Phillip softly smiled. "Yeah, guess so."

"I like to think her spirit's still out there. In the forest and in the field with you."

Phillip stared at their aunt in the white casket, her face resting in eternal peace.

"I was talking to Mom and Dad recently," Lauren said. "They were telling me about your hospital visits in Atlanta."

"What'd they say?" Phillip growled.

"Only how the NFL is making it so hard on you. I haven't told anyone. I know that's your business."

Phillip leaned back, his shoulders relaxing.

"You sacrificed everything. I really hope they do the right thing now."

"They're not going to."

"They told you that?" Lauren asked.

"They're not giving me anything," Phillip muttered.

Lauren clasped her hands together. "That's terrible, Phillip. I'm so sorry."

Phillip rested his hand on her shoulder as he stood up.

"I'm gunna get some air," Phillip said, sliding past her. He pushed open the funeral home doors, leaving the white chapel behind.

A TEMPEST OF BLACK WAVES raged in Phillip. Alone in his bedroom, he wore a black sweatshirt and camouflage pants. He picked up his iPhone and can of Skoal and tucked them into his front sweatshirt pocket.

He dumped a handful of prescription pills and kratom capsules into his hand, washing them down with a liquid kratom shot. He opened his closet and picked up a black motorcycle helmet off the top shelf. He slid it over his head, the tinted visor blacking out his face.

The tempest of black waves drove him out of his bedroom and through the empty house. Outside, he mounted his four-wheeler, fired it up, and cut out of the driveway.

He rode west down Marshall Road, staying on his route past the open field and white fences of the wealthy few. On the right side of the road, he reached the brown, wooden-beam fence leading to the stone archway of the Lesslie private drive.

He rode past the Lesslie entrance, the fence running past a large, wooden cross guarding their estate. He turned right past the wooden cross where the fence ended onto a narrow, dirt path running along the forest surrounding the private property. The tires of the four-wheeler pounded down the hidden terrain, winding deep into the woods, until the fence re-emerged next to the trail.

He parked next to the wooden beams and dismounted his four-wheeler. Across the fence, he surveyed the green forest enshrouding the Lesslie estate. Through a clearing, he spotted a dirt footpath between the trees.

He hoisted himself over the fence, and marched down the dirt footpath with stealth, descending through the forest. Near the forest's edge, the trees thinned out, giving way to a large, grassy backyard behind the sprawling, brick mansion.

The excitement of children's voices rang across the backyard, forcing him to hide behind a tree near the end of the footpath. He peered around the trunk and spotted the Lesslie family gathered near their man-made pond in the backyard.

Jeff Lesslie, a lean, middle-aged white man with matching brown hair and beard, stood next to his wife, Katie Lesslie, a thin, middle-aged white woman with long, brown hair.

They watched over their daughter, Adah Lesslie, a cheery, nine-year-old girl, and their son, Noah Lesslie, an inquisitive, five-year-old boy, crouching near the end of the pond. Adah pointed to a koi fish, and Noah clapped with delight.

Behind them, sitting under a shaded porch swing, Doctor Robert Lesslie, a lean, elderly white man with matching white hair and beard, rocked back and forth with his wife, Barbara Lesslie, a thin, elderly white woman with short, white hair.

The dark figure studied them. The tempest of black waves surged under his black motorcycle helmet. He faded back into the trees, disappearing into the forest.

XV

On April 6, 2021, a mild Tuesday in Miami, Ashley, halfway to term in her white sundress, monitored P.J. He ate a bowl of Cheerios in their hotel room in a matching aqua-and-orange Miami Dolphins tank top and shorts. Allen, wearing a black-and-red Miami Heat T-shirt and blue jeans, swung the hotel door open waving three zoo passes in his hand.

"Who's ready to go to the zoo?"

Allen and Ashley waited for P.J., but he set his spoon down in his cereal bowl, hanging his head. Ashley lowered herself down into the seat next to him, rubbing his back.

"What's the matter, baby? I thought you wanted to go to the zoo?"

"I do."

"You don't seem like it."

"I miss Dad."

Ashley leaned forward and hugged him. "I'm sorry, baby. I know you do." Ashley let go and sat back up. "You can call him when we get back home. Okay?"

"Can I call him now?"

Ashley looked over at Allen who shrugged.

"Fine with me," Allen said.

"Please?" P.J. begged.

"We can try," Ashley said, "but don't get too excited. I

don't know if he'll answer."

"Can we FaceTime him?"

"Sure," Ashley sighed.

P.J. shot out of his chair and picked up Ashley's iPhone on the nightstand, handing it to her. Ashley placed a FaceTime call to Phillip, tensing with each ring while Phillip's name lit up the screen.

"Hello?" Phillip said, his face replacing his name on-screen, the Carolina Panthers poster growling behind him in his bedroom.

"Hi, Phil," Ashley said, "I'm with P.J. in Miami. You have a minute to talk with him quick?"

"Yeah, put him on."

Ashley handed P.J. the phone, bouncing with excitement.

"Hi, Dad!"

"Hey, buddy," Phillip said, gently smiling. "Are you having fun on vacation?"

"Yeah, it's lots of fun."

"What have you been doing?"

"Yesterday we went to the beach," P.J. said, "and I swam in the ocean."

"Wow, that's so cool. What are you doing today?"

"We're going to the zoo."

"I love the zoo," Phillip said. "What do you wanna see the most?"

"Parrots," P.J. said.

"Really?" Phillip asked. "What do you like about parrots?"

"I like their different colors."

"They are pretty birds."

Ashley reached out and rubbed P.J.'s back.

"All right, baby," Ashley said. "We need to get going so we can see all the animals. Say goodbye to your Dad."

P.J. lifted one hand, waving to him. "Bye, Dad."

Phillip raised his hand back, waving goodbye. "I love you, buddy. I'll talk to you later."

Ashley took the phone back and ended the call, a black screen replacing Phillip's face.

"Feel better?" Ashley asked.

"Yeah," P.J. said.

The next day, on Wednesday, April 7, 2021, Alonzo called Scott Casterline from his porch. The phone rang while the trees swayed in the wind, the leaves rustling together, until it went to voicemail.

"Hey there, Scott, this is Alonzo Adams callin about Phillip. If you'd give me a call back I'd sure appreciate it."

Alonzo stooped back inside through the kitchen door to Phyllis. Disappointment hung over him as he sat down at the kitchen table, leaning toward her.

"I left a voicemail," Alonzo whispered. "I'm sure he'll call me back."

"I sure hope so," Phyllis whispered. "He's hardly come out of his room since Easter. I'm all out of ideas."

"We better get a move on," Alonzo whispered. "I'll go tell him we're leavin."

Alonzo shuffled down the hallway toward Phillip's closed bedroom door.

In his bedroom, Phillip, wearing a black sweatshirt and

camouflage pants over his work boots, punched in the code to his gun safe and swung the door open.

Alonzo thumped on the door. "Phil?"

Phillip's demented eyes flared.

"Your mama and I are headed up to Gastonia to see her sister. Give us a holler if you need us."

Phillip waited while Alonzo's footsteps faded down the hallway, the house falling silent. The white minivan puttered out of the driveway and down Marshall Road.

Phillip scanned over his small armory of handguns and rifles. A hurricane of black waves howled inside of him. He grabbed the Kriss Vector with a drum magazine and the MP5 submachine gun, slinging them over his shoulders in a metal cross. The violent cyclone pulled him under the deadly waters, sinking into the darkness.

He grabbed a small, red pouch filled with ammunition, strapping it around his waist under his black sweatshirt. The hurricane raged inside of him, washing away the last light of consciousness.

He closed the gun safe, thudding back over to his desk. He snatched his dark-red iPhone and blue can of Skoal, stuffing them into his front sweatshirt pocket. Phillip poured a handful of prescription pills and kratom capsules into his hand, washing them down with a shot of liquid kratom. The sedatives diffused into his bloodstream, cooling the inferno of inflammation burning throughout his body.

He opened his closet and pulled down his black motorcycle helmet. He slid it on, becoming the hurricane. Phillip Adams drowned under the black waves. Only the disease remained.

He marched out of his bedroom and through the quiet house. On his way out the front door, the reflection of the wooden cross on the living room wall warped across his black motorcycle helmet.

In the driveway, he mounted his four-wheeler and roared west down Marshall Road. He accelerated past the open field, throttling the four-wheeler as he sped past the white fences and towering trees protecting the countryside elite.

On the right side of the road, he reached the brown, wooden-beam fence and stone archway of the Lesslie estate. He roared past it, letting off the throttle as he reached the large, wooden cross. He cut right down the narrow, dirt path leading into the forest surrounding the Lesslie estate.

He careened down the winding path until he reached his hidden entrance, parking next to the fence. He leapt off his four-wheeler and pulled around the Kriss Vector semiautomatic rifle, clutching it in his hands as he hurdled the fence.

He charged down the dirt footpath, descending through the forest with focused precision. A hurricane of black waves making landfall.

David Fudge, the elderly white groundskeeper, in a wide-brimmed hat and old pair of overalls, sheared the long grass on the far side of the backyard. The tall trees sheltered him from the cyclone of death storming out of the forest.

Phillip sprinted past the man-made pond, toward the backside of the sprawling, brick mansion. He charged around the side wall, his rifle raised, as he emerged onto the grand, front entrance of the mansion.

On the inside of the gated driveway, two heating and air

conditioning workers, James Lewis and Robert Shook, white men in their mid-thirties, unloaded supplies from the back of their red-and-white service truck.

Phillip aimed at James Lewis, his petrified eyes transfixed on the rifle as a burst of bullets exploded out of the drum magazine. Dark blood stains seeped across his bright-red service uniform as he collapsed on the ground.

Robert Shook froze as Phillip aimed at him, a second burst of bullets ripping through his chest and shattering his jaw. He collapsed on the driveway next to his dead co-worker, Phillip looming over them as they bled out on the concrete.

Phillip sprinted toward the house, swinging the Kriss Vector back over his shoulder, and whipping around his fully loaded MP5 submachine gun. He reached the front door, but it was deadbolted shut.

Small glass panes lined the wall on the left side of the door. He lifted the butt of his gun, smashing it into them until they cracked and shattered. As he knocked out the glass, his dark-red iPhone and blue can of Skoal tumbled out of his sweatshirt pocket, falling on the ground next to the steps.

He reached his hand in through the open pane, his sweatshirt protecting his arm from the shards of glass, and unlocked the deadbolt. He threw the front door open, charging into the foyer.

He swept through the silent living room, kitchen, and dining room, the barrel of his submachine gun aimed straight ahead and ready to fire. He finished a sweep of the first floor when he reached a back hallway. At the far end, a closed door muffled children crying. He charged toward the door, slamming his shoulder into it until the door to a home gym exploded open and he rushed inside.

Doctor Robert Lesslie held his screaming granddaughter, Adah Lesslie, while Barbara Lesslie held their crying grandson, Noah Lesslie.

"Please!" Doctor Lesslie screamed. "Don't hurt the children!"

A spray of bullets burst out of the submachine gun, slaughtering the Lesslie family. The man in the black motorcycle helmet stood over their dying bodies, their blood mixing together on the wooden floor.

He left them lying together lifeless as he charged back out of the room. He sprinted back through the first floor of the house, unzipping his red ammo pouch as he reached the front door.

Bleeding out, Robert Shook lay on the ground in the driveway while Phillip reloaded his MP5. He zipped the red ammo pouch shut, and stormed back into the foyer.

In the living room, he reached a staircase and marched up the stairs, reaching a long hallway. Down the hallway full of open rooms, the closed master bedroom door concealed the whines of a whimpering dog.

He aimed his gun at the door and marched toward it. He positioned his hand on the doorknob and threw it open. Inside, a golden retriever curled in a corner next to the bed, whimpering from the gunshots. He aimed the gun at the dog while it cried in the corner.

His black motorcycle helmet swept from left to right across the room, searching for the rest of the Lesslie family. He tilted the barrel up toward the ceiling, leaving the dog alone. He marched back into the hallway and closed the door.

He swept through the remaining rooms, finding the second floor empty of human life. He charged back down the steps and out the front door, leaving behind a massacre.

He threw the MP5 back over his shoulder and sprinted past Robert Shook. Once Phillip disappeared around the mansion, Robert Shook, covered in blood, dragged himself up the driveway to the driver's door of his work van.

He reached up and tugged at the door handle, cracking the door open. Lying on the ground, he dug in the door pocket and pulled out his cell phone. He clicked on contacts, calling his manager.

"Help me," he slurred with a broken jaw, "we've been shot."

In the backyard, Phillip fled through the open grass, vanishing into the forest. On the far side of the backyard, David Fudge, hiding behind the trees, held his cell phone up.

"9-1-1," a female dispatcher answered.

"Yes, ma'am," David answered in a Southern drawl, "I think we've had some trouble on Marshall Road."

"What's goin on at Marshall Road?"

"I think there's been a bad shooting."

Phillip sprinted through the forest up the dirt footpath, hurdling over the fence. He lunged onto his four-wheeler, fired it up, and careened back down the winding forest path.

He roared back home down Marshall Road, accelerating to full speed as he passed the white fences of the nearby neighbors. Once he reached the open field, the sound of sirens wailed in the distance.

As he cut up his driveway, he drove the four-wheeler

behind the house. As he leapt off, the whirring blades of a black police helicopter hovered overhead. He rushed inside the porch as the wailing sirens grew louder.

He unstrapped his rifles and hid them under the old couch tucked in the corner. He slid off his black motorcycle helmet, placing it on the porch table. He opened the kitchen door and crept into the empty house.

The police helicopter flew over Marshall Road searching for the assailant. The flashing sirens of police vehicles lined the Lesslie estate from the stone archway to James Lewis's body, lying dead on the ground next to his red-and-white service vehicle.

Near the entrance, David Fudge recounted his story to detectives as they jotted down notes. Police officers searched the front of the house, finding shell casings on the ground, while others spread out through the backyard, wading into the forest.

Inside the home gym, York County Sheriff Kevin Tolson, a stern, middle-aged white man with a shaved head, stood over the deceased Lesslie family. Their skin drained pale white as they lay in a dark-red pool of blood.

Deputy Ryan Quinn filed into the room disgusted and confused. "I don't know what to make of it."

Sheriff Tolson shifted away from the bodies. "What's the status on the sixth victim?"

"He's in critical condition. Doesn't sound like he's going to live."

A young male officer hurried into the room, holding Phillip's dark-red iPhone and blue can of Skoal.

"I just found these outside on the ground by the broken panes of glass. I think the shooter dropped them."

"Get that down to the lab," Sheriff Tolson said. "I want the number off that cell phone ASAP."

That night, Alonzo pulled into the driveway, parking the white minivan in the garage. He helped lower Phyllis down out of the vehicle, and she drove up the ramp into the kitchen. Inside the quiet house, he followed her into their bedroom, closing the door behind him.

"Let me get you tucked in, sweetie," Alonzo said. "I might watch a little somethin on TV before I turn in."

"Thank you, dear," Phyllis said.

In his bedroom, Phillip stood holding a pistol to his chest. His wild eyes tracked the footsteps approaching down the hallway. Alonzo knocked on the door and Phillip aimed at the sound.

"Phil," Alonzo called out, "we're back home."

Phillip kept the gun aimed at the door, remaining silent, until Alonzo shuffled back down the hallway.

In the living room, Alonzo sank into the sofa. He grabbed the television remote when a spotlight flooded the living room window, shining through the soft, green blinds.

Alonzo pushed himself off the sofa, creeping toward the door. Outside, stomping boots made him tense with flashbacks from his service in the U.S. Army. He swung the door open, revealing a swarm of SWAT team members in black tactical gear aiming their guns at him.

In his driveway, the York County BearCat, a large,

armored vehicle, aimed its spotlight on Alonzo. In his neighbor's driveway, an M.R.A.P. — Mine Resistant Ambush Protection vehicle — an enormous, armored machine, flooded Alonzo's backyard with a spotlight.

"Hands up!"

"On your knees!"

Alonzo raised his hands above his head, wincing from the pain as he landed on his knees. One SWAT member lowered his gun and whipped out his handcuffs. He wrenched Alonzo's wrists behind his back and pulled him to his feet.

"On your feet! Move!" he shouted.

Alonzo stumbled forward in disbelief. "What's goin on?" Alonzo asked. "What happened?"

The SWAT member shoved Alonzo forward until they reached the road. A police car waited for them with the back door open. The SWAT member forced Alonzo into the backseat, slamming the door shut.

The Rock Hill police officer driving the car turned on the red-and-blue emergency lights, speeding off west down Marshall Road. As he passed through the police barricade, Alonzo kicked at his seat.

"Hey now, what's goin on?! My wife and son are in there!"

"You can confirm that?" the officer asked.

"Yes! And my wife is paralyzed so you need to be careful!"

The police officer picked up his radio as he passed the open field. "Suspect's father confirms suspect and suspect's mother are inside. Suspect's mother is paralyzed."

"Suspect?" Alonzo asked. "Are you talkin about Phil?"

"Where are they in the house?"

"My wife is in the first bedroom down the hallway. And Phil is in the back bedroom."

The officer relayed the information as he drove by the white fences glowing red-and-blue from his lights. Ahead, as they reached the brown, wooden-beam fence, a row of red-and-blue lights from the squad cars lit up the black night sky.

In the back of the BearCat, Detective Tolson grabbed the radio microphone for the loudspeakers, his voice booming across Marshall Road. "Phillip Adams, this is the police. We have you surrounded. Come out with your hands up."

In his bedroom, Phillip swung his gun from the door to the window. Down the hallway, Phyllis lay in the dark, trapped in her bed.

"Alonzo!" Phyllis screamed.

Next door, Deputy Quinn ushered Duane out of his house, staggering past the massive military vehicle in his driveway.

"What's happening?" Duane stammered.

"We need you to clear the area immediately," Deputy Quinn instructed. "We have an active shooter next door."

"Phil?"

"Please, sir, we need you to clear the area now."

Deputy Quinn led him safely down the road, past the BearCat booming from Detective Tolson's voice.

"I repeat, Phillip Adams, we have you surrounded. Come out with your hands up."

The front door hung open, the BearCat's spotlight shining into the living room.

As the silent standoff dragged into the night, Detective Tolson looked to the SWAT leader in the back of the BearCat.

"We need to get the suspect's mother. Let's move."

The SWAT leader nodded and they filed out the back of the BearCat. On the sheltered side of the armored vehicle, they lined up in stack formation. The SWAT leader held his shield in front, while the following SWAT members aimed their guns forward, ending with Detective Tolson in back. They marched forward into the living room.

Inside they broke up, sweeping through the quiet living room and kitchen. Detective Tolson walked to the edge of the dark hallway with his gun aimed at the closed back door.

"Phillip Adams? You hear me?"

Inside his bedroom, Phillip, seized with dementia, aimed the gun at the door.

From her bed, Phyllis cried in silent terror, stuck between their standoff.

Detective Tolson nodded to the front door. "Bring in Big Boy," he whispered.

The SWAT leader left, returning with a Rock Hill bomb squad member, driving a small tank on tracked wheels with an attached, retractable claw. The bomb squad member held a remote control with a monitor in the center, displaying the robot's visuals.

Detective Tolson pointed with his gun to the first closed door, and the small tank rolled down the dark hallway. Its claw reached out, grabbing the doorknob and twisting the door open.

Its front light powered on, shining a light on Phyllis

trapped in her bed. She lifted her hands toward the light. "Please don't shoot," Phyllis cried.

From the monitor, the bomb squad member spotted her hands in the air. "Located suspect's mother."

A SWAT member swooped into her bedroom, scooping Phyllis into his arms, and whisking her out of the bedroom. Phyllis shuddered as he rushed her past the team of SWAT members in her kitchen, living room, and sprawling across her front yard.

Inside the house, Big Boy backed up into the hallway and rolled toward Phillip's bedroom door. Its light illuminated the path forward, rolling past P.J.'s open bedroom door. Detective Tolson crept behind the small tank with his gun drawn. He peered into P.J.'s bedroom, the ghost of a young Michael Jordan hovering in the darkness.

Big Boy stopped at Phillip's bedroom door, Detective Tolson crouching behind the small tank. Phillip aimed his gun at the door, ready to fire at the approaching sound. The retractable claw reached out, grabbing the doorknob and twisting the door open.

Phillip tilted the gun back, his hands trembling as he shoved the barrel of the gun into his mouth. Phillip pulled the trigger, the bullet shattering through the back of his skull. He collapsed on the ground in front of the door, his blood blending into the dark-red carpet.

The claw pushed the door open until it hit Phillip's dead body. Detective Tolson slid in through the opening, discovering Phillip under his feet.

"Suspect is deceased."

On the soft sand of Miami Beach, Ashley reclined in a dark-red one-piece swimsuit in a blue beach chair under a matching blue umbrella. P.J. swam with Allen in the water, the light-blue sky blending into the dark-blue ocean.

From her straw purse, Ashley's iPhone rang with an incoming call. She sat up and dug it out, her concern growing as she answered Alonzo's call.

"Hello?" Ashley asked.

"Hi there, Ashley," Alonzo rasped. "I need to talk to you. It's about Phillip."

"What's the matter?"

"He did somethin real, real bad."

"What?"

"They say he went and shot some people. A doctor and his family. Then he took his own life."

Ashley's mouth hung open, reeling from shock. "What? Why?"

"I don't know. Nobody does."

"That doesn't make sense. Phillip wouldn't hurt anybody."

"They found his notebooks," Alonzo said. "They were askin if he's in some kind of cult. But I said he'd never get caught up in somethin like that."

"He's always written in those notebooks," Ashley said. "I just can't believe it."

"All I can say is he was a good kid. And I think football messed him up."

XVI

ON A WARM SUNDAY, ONE week after Easter, hundreds from the community gathered at Fountain Park in Rock Hill. The evening sun shined on the attendees in bright shirts to honor the bright lights Adah and Noah Lesslie shined on the world.

Behind the crowd the giant stone fountain sprayed white water from its center spout, misting the air over the gathering. In front of them, gray beams arced over the top of the concrete stage in a metal rainbow.

In the back of the stage, Jamey Dagenhart, a thin white man with curly brown hair and a goatee, unstrapped his acoustic guitar, resting it on the stand as his bandmates settled into position. He stepped up to the center podium before the colorful crowd. Jeff and Katie Lesslie sat in the front row, surrounded by their surviving family members.

"Good evening," Jamey announced. "On behalf of the Lesslie family, I want to thank you for coming to this memorial service and prayer vigil tonight. My name is Jamey Dagenhart, and I'm an elder at first ARP where they attend worship. We've gathered here to give God thanks for life. And for the lives of Robert and Barbara and Adah and Noah Lesslie."

Jeff glanced at Katie, their spirits rising in their chests, softly smiling together.

For over an hour, friends and family of the Lesslies took turns at the podium, recounting how much joy the Lesslies brought them. They sang hymns and prayed for the Lesslie family and the families of James Lewis and Robert Shook. Jeff and Katie drank in each eulogy as the fountain's mist spread over the crowd.

Under the metal rainbow, Amy Lesslie Klobuk, a white woman with curly brown hair, took the stage. Beside her stood Lori Lesslie Alexander, a white woman with long blonde hair, and Rodney Lesslie, a tall white man with sandy brown hair.

"What a beautiful day," remarked Amy. "We're Amy Klobuk, Lori Alexander, and Rodney Lesslie. Together with Jeff, we're the children of Robert and Barbara. And the three of us up here get to call ourselves aunts and uncle to Adah and Noah."

Jeff held Katie's hand as tears streamed down her face.

"Adah Lesslie inherited a love of music from both sides of her family," Amy said into the microphone. "And her parents discovered in the last few days she wrote a song. I'm not going to sing it—" a soft laughter rang throughout the crowd "—but I will read it to you exactly as it's written. It's called 'You and Me.'"

You and me, we can love one another, even through the hardest times, even through the darkest days. We can love one another, even in the deepest fog, we will find one another and love each other. When people see us, they will see Jesus Christ in you and me. Oh, oh, oooh, oh, oh, oooh.

Katie laughed, wiping her tears away as Jeff laughed with her, Adah's song alive for the first time.

Ashley waded through her hallway, adorned in a black shawl and dress, into P.J.'s bedroom. Her pregnancy weighed down her body. Phillip's death weighed down her mind. P.J. sat on the edge of his bed in a long-sleeved black shirt and black jeans. He held a white coaster made of clay when Ashley sat down next to him, gently rubbing his back.

"All right, P.J.," Ashley said, "it's almost time to go. But we don't have to. It's your choice."

"I want to see Dad," P.J. said.

"Remember, it's going to look like he's sleeping. He can't talk to you, but you can talk to him. Understand?"

"I understand."

"What do you have there?"

"I made this for Dad in art class for Father's Day. Can I give it to him?"

P.J. held up the white coaster, his handprint in the center with the words "I love you Dad" wrapping around the palm.

"Of course, baby," Ashley said. "I know he would love it."

On the drive to Rock Hill, Ashley considered how P.J.'s life in the area would change. She crossed the bridge over the Catawba River, realizing Phillip blackened the water for him and their son, Phillip Adams Junior.

She took the exit for his funeral, the hostility increasing as she reached AME Zion Church. Protesters and police officers in patrol cars surrounded the red-brick house of worship with a white steeple. Ashley nudged her car through the protesters until she reached a police officer guarding the parking lot entrance. She rolled down her window while the officer profiled her.

"Are you immediate family?" the officer asked.

"Yes. I have his son in the backseat."

The officer examined P.J. in his Iron Man booster seat, nodding and stepping aside.

"Go on in."

Ashley pulled into the parking lot, parking next to Alonzo and Phyllis's minivan. She slid out of the car and unstrapped P.J., the church looming in silence next to the thundering mob of protesters in the street. Ashley opened the white church door for P.J. carrying his white clay coaster.

In the lobby, Alonzo stood next to Phyllis in her wheelchair, both dressed in black. P.J. sprinted up to his grandparents, Alonzo crouching down to hug him.

"Papa!" P.J. shouted.

"There he is," Alonzo said, softly smiling.

Phyllis reached out for P.J., and he embraced her in a hug.

"There's my sweet, little boy," Phyllis said.

Alonzo bowed his head to Ashley as she approached.

"We appreciate you comin with P.J.," Alonzo said. "We know it would have meant a lot to Phil."

"P.J. wanted to come," Ashley said. "He wants to see his Dad."

"He's in there," Phyllis said. "You can go see him if you're ready."

Ashley rubbed P.J.'s back. "Ready?"

P.J. held Ashley's hand as they entered the small white chapel. Under a large, wooden cross at the altar, Phillip lay in a black casket wearing a black suit and tie. His face frozen in death, the black waves inside of him hardened to ice.

Dwight, Lauren, and Ryan sat with their families in the wooden pews, glancing up as Ashley led P.J. to Phillip. As they approached the altar, P.J. stood just taller than Phillip in his casket, their faces almost touching. Tears trickled down Ashley's cheeks as P.J. absorbed his father's death.

"Here he is, baby," Ashley said. "If you want to tell him something, now is the time."

"Bye, Dad. I love you."

"He loves you too, baby. He loves you too."

P.J. lifted the clay coaster, setting it on his chest. P.J.'s handprint replaced Phillip's beating heart.

IN JUNE, THE HOTEL ELEVATOR doors opened and Phyllis drove out into the lobby, Alonzo following her as the elevator doors closed. In the parking lot, they pulled out into traffic and made their way back to their quiet corner of Rock Hill.

On their way down Marshall Road, they passed the Lesslie estate, the large, wooden cross guarding the abandoned paradise. The shade of the green tree leaves hung over the wooden-beam fence, replacing the red-and-blue police presence.

They passed the white fences and rows of trees walling off their wealthy neighbors from the memories of Marshall Road. In the open field, the tall grass swayed from a breeze under the summer sun.

In his driveway, Alonzo parked his minivan next to another white construction van. A blue dumpster filled with debris rested next to Phillip's Camaro and four-wheeler covered in black tarps. Alonzo rolled down his driver's window as a young crew worker came out of the house, tossing a piece of Phillip's dark-red carpet into the dumpster.

"How's it goin today?" Alonzo asked.

"We're gettin the new carpet installed in the back bedroom. Wanna come see?"

"Nah, that's fine. Was just passin through and wanted to check in."

"We're gunna have this place lookin brand new, Mr. Adams. Won't even recognize it when we're done."

Alonzo softly nodded. "I won't keep you. Carry on."

Alonzo rolled the window up as the crew worker headed back inside. Alonzo backed out of the driveway and drove toward Charlotte, his home fading in the rearview mirror.

That afternoon, P.J. played tag in a park with other children, wearing his dad's red jersey over a blue T-shirt. He darted across the jungle gym as another boy tried to tag him. Ashley sat on a nearby park bench with Alonzo and Phyllis, her eyes hidden under black sunglasses.

"I appreciate you two seeing P.J. so much," Ashley said. "I can tell it's been helping him process everything."

"Of course," Phyllis said. "We want him to know we'll always be there for him."

"That's right," Alonzo said, "we'll help the boy any way we can."

"Thank you, both," Ashley said. "The therapy is helping

him too. But he's just so young. I still don't think he fully understands."

"I was saying to Alonzo I should start therapy," Phyllis said. "It might do me some good to talk to someone too."

"Truth is," Alonzo said, "after we get the house all fixed up, we might put it up for sale."

"Really?" Ashley asked.

"Just thinkin about it. Nothin set in stone yet."

"I'm not sure I can stay in the area anymore," Phyllis sighed. "But that was our home for so long. I just don't know."

"I've been talking with Allen," Ashley said. "We're not sure we can stay here either. Thought it might be best for P.J. to get away from here."

"Where you thinkin about goin?" Alonzo asked.

"Allen's from Winston-Salem. We thought that might be a nice place to start over." Ashley rubbed her pregnant stomach. "Especially with the little one on the way."

"Listen to your heart," Phyllis said. "A mother knows what's best for her children."

P.J. chased a little boy around the slide, tagging him on the shoulder before climbing up the jungle gym.

"He was supposed to be in a summer football camp," Ashley said. "I told him it was canceled, but I don't think he believed me."

"I don't blame you," Alonzo said. "I'm kickin myself for givin him that jersey."

"I told him he could play in the fall, but I don't think I can let him play football again," Ashley said.

P.J. slid down the slide as the little boy chased him. The little boy's fingers grasped at P.J.'s jersey as he escaped untouched.

"Phillip Adams had an extraordinary amount of CTE pathology in the frontal lobe, the area of the brain behind the forehead. Frontal lobe damage is associated with violent, impulsive or explosive behavior, a 'short fuse,' and a lack of self-control." — Dr. Ann McKee, Director of the Boston University CTE Center.

The FBI cited Dr. Ann McKee in the official conclusion of their report. No motive for the murders was ever determined.

In 2023 and 2024, Alonzo Adams sued the NFL and South Carolina State University, Phillip's alma mater, for the wrongful death of his son. As of 2025, the case is still ongoing.

ABOUT THE AUTHOR

PIERCE DE BAUCHE IS A novelist and screenwriter with a Bachelor's degree in Communication Arts: Radio, Television, and Film from the University of Wisconsin-Madison. Born and raised in Wisconsin, he is a proud Green Bay Packers fan whose passion for the sport and concern for the health of the players inspired *Under the Black Waves*.

www.ingramcontent.com/pod-product-compliance
Lightning Source LLC
Chambersburg PA
CBHW020550030426
42337CB00013B/1027